Educational Psychology of Srimad Bhagavad Gita

Educational Psychology of Srimad Bhagavad Gita

by

Chandra Shekhar Pandey

Indian Council of Social Science Research

MLBD PUBLICATIONS

Motilal Banarsidass Publications

First published in 2025

Published by
INDIAN COUNCIL OF SOCIAL SCIENCE RESEARCH
(Ministry of Education), Government of India,
Aruna Asaf Ali Marg, New Delhi – 110067.
Phone: 9220521105
Email: prsdivision@icssr.org • Website: www.icssr.org

In association with
MOTILAL BANARSIDASS
PUBLICATIONS
4741/23, Ansari Road, Daryaganj, New Delhi - 110002 (India)
Email: mlbd@mlbd.com | sales@mlbd.com
exports@mlbd.com | publications@mlbd.com
Website: www.mlbd.com

ISBN : 978-81-979177-4-5 (HB)

Printed and bound in India

Contents

Acknowledgment

The search for knowledge and meaning is an infinite journey, and when it enters the realm of the Srimad Bhagavad Gita—the treasure trove of Indian spirituality—it becomes truly endless. When I call it a never-ending journey, I mean that true knowledge is a process of continuous discovery. From the perspective of learning, it is ever-evolving. I thank Shri Krishna for the inspiration to undertake the meaningful work of bringing the essence of the Gita to the understanding of human behaviour from a psychological perspective.

I express my heartfelt gratitude to all those who have contributed to the completion of this work. First and foremost, I would like to thank my supervisor, Prof. Dr. Sanjay Sonker, for providing me with invaluable guidance and support throughout the course of this research. I would also like to extend my gratitude to ICSSR, New Delhi, for its prompt administrative support and provision of resources. My sincere thanks also go to my colleagues and peers who have provided valuable feedback and support throughout the research process. Your encouragement and inspiration have been a source of motivation and strength for me. I would like to express my gratitude to the staff and faculty of BHU for providing the necessary resources and facilities for carrying out this research. I am deeply indebted to my father — Shri Lal Jee Pandey, and mother — Shrimati Dharmavati Devi, for their unwavering support and encouragement. Their love and encouragement have been a constant source of inspiration and motivation.

Dr. Chandra Shekhar Pandey.

Preface

This work is the result of my postdoctoral research, sponsored by ICSSR, New Delhi, in association with Banaras Hindu University. The curiosity to know thyself has been a constant source of inspiration for mankind for ages, across cultures and history. Greek culture and Indian culture have both admired the effort to understand the true self of a person. This is where the discourse should start in spirituality, education, and social life. Without understanding oneself, one cannot achieve true wisdom and knowledge of reality. The concept of man is the cornerstone of any education system. This work attempts to understand the concept of man, his behavior, and his thought processes as described by the Srimad Bhagavad Gita in its verses. By providing an overview of foundational research, the book is divided into several sections. It presents studies on the educational relevance of religious texts around the world, a brief methodological approach, and identifies principles of educational psychology applied in the context of the Srimad Bhagavad Gita. After identifying the relevant theories and principles of educational psychology, the main concepts are elaborated, explained, and interpreted in the context of modern psychology. Concepts of emotional intelligence, mindfulness, self-awareness, the concept of self, and self-regulation are described in detail. Furthermore, this study proposes a unique model of the psychological process of desire. This work also encompasses the development of psychometric instruments for measuring the concept of life satisfaction and leadership. Dimensions of Resolute Intelligence are also identified. Lastly, the study explores andragogical principles in the context of the Srimad Bhagavad Gita.

Despite my sincere efforts, this work may have its limitations due to the vastness and depth of the Srimad Bhagavad Gita and its ever-evolving multidisciplinary impact on different knowledge systems. This work is but a humble attempt to apply ancient wisdom to understand human behaviour and cognition in educational context. I welcome constructive feedback and further discussion that would help refine and expand these ideas.

Dr. Chandra Shekhar Pandey

List of Tables

List of Figures

CHAPTER 1
Introduction

The Srimad Bhagavad Gita is an ancient Hindu scripture. It contains the teachings of Lord Krishna to his disciple, and friend Arjuna on the battlefield of Kurukshetra. Kurukshetra is the pious land of a battle between virtue and vice; Dharma and Adharma. The concept of "Kshetra" is very important in Gita. Krishna says that the body itself is a Kshetra — A field of sown impressions, experiences, actions and interactions with the society. Some expositions on Gita take this view very seriously and work on the cognitive interpretations of the scripture, in which all the Mahabharata actors are within the playground of human body and psyche.

Gita could be described as a comprehensive guide for human society, life and consciousness. It addresses various aspects of human life, society and its manifestations. Not a single aspect of human life is untouched by the interpretations of Gita. It addresses almost all aspects of human existence, including spirituality, ethics, morality and duty of individual. The inseparability of Gita's scope from human life makes it one of the most important texts for education and educational psychology which are directly concerned about younger generations future life goals and harmonious living in today's society.

Educational psychology applies the theories and psychological principles for enhancing the structured formal educational processes and curricular experiences. Learning is a collaborative and interactive process involving student and teacher, both in the process of knowledge creation and dissemination. In educational psychology, teachers use principles of learning, behavioral change, motivation etc. for enhancing the educational process. In the same manner, Gita can be studied from the perspective of educational psychology which tries to explore the educational and psychological processes undergoing and influencing the learning and knowledge acquisition processes. Krishna serves as a friend of Arjuna, a philosopher friend and a concerned guide who leads the paths of his disciple for a determined course of action — Dharma, the greatest duty of a human being.

Srimad Bhagavad Gita is considered the essence of Upanishads. The popular metaphor of Krishna as milkman, Upanaishadas as Cow, Arjnua as a Calf; and Gita as milk indicate the fact that the text is one of the foundational significances in philosophical discourse of Indian philosophy, theology, and psychology. The verses of Gita serve as models of human behavior in the extreme conditions of war. For Gita, War is ongoing in the human psyche and by epistemic capabilities of resolute intelligence, and individual could resolve it. Krishna guides arjuna in actual battlefield situations. What could be more practical approach than guiding in real crisis demanding a decisions to stand for justice. For Gita, war of Mahabharata is a curriculum of life. Krishna prepares Arjuna to make decisions for broader wellbeing of society and greater values. Arjuna had to fight with his own kin and teachers and Krishna prepares him for this immense difficult situation. Through this process, Arjuna learns to control his basic instincts of fear and love.

He acquires the skill of emotional management and decision making and overcome the anxieties related to his own psyche. Sanjay, as a non-participant observer, observes, summarizes and explains the events of the Kurukshetra battlefield to Dhritarashtra.

The Gita's emphasis on self-knowledge and self-realization as the first principle of gaining knowledge, is generally inclined with the Indian philosophical tradition. Self-knowledge and self-realization are considered as the foundation for all knowledge and action. Lord Krishna tells Arjuna, "Know your true self, and then take action". Self-knowledge comes from inner reflection, contemplation, and meditation. It is not only intellectual knowledge but experiential knowledge gained through meditation, contemplation and inner reflection. Self-knowledge results in self-realization with awareness of one's true nature as an eternal and infinite being beyond the body and physical limitations. This realization helps in transcendence of ego, redemption from the cycle of birth and death, and leads to liberation or moksha.

The relevance of self-knowledge and self-realization to education is evident in various educational philosophies, approaches and methodologies. For instance, the Indian philosopher Jiddu Krishnamurti has emphasized the importance of self-knowledge and discovery in education. This emphasis on self-discovery and knowledge is also reflected in western perspectives. Know thyself was inscribed in Apollo's temple near 600 BC. The basis of all knowledge as self-knowledge is a fundamental tenet of almost all philosophical schools. Generally, philosophers who believe in a systematic and relatively stable nature of knowledge has a general tendency of accepting human self as a stable and knowable entity. Eastern philosophers and thoughts believe in the concept of "Atma" which is immutable, atomic, stable, omnipresent god as the ultimate source of knowledge. Western philosophers like Plato also emphasized self as source of all knowledge. The purpose of education is not to imitate anything or anyone. The purpose of education is to be yourself at all times, because you are always expected to follow something in order to be virtuous and earn respect in this society (Krishnamurti, 1953).

Similarly, Experiential learning has been emphasized by American philosopher and educator John Dewey who believed that education should be focused on developing whole personality of the person and learning should be connected to real life experiences. A sense of purpose and direction is to be fostered by education. This pragmatic purposivism in philosophy is indicative of the discourse of aims and goals of education. It also gives an insight about purposiveness of education and connects it to the practical solutions of life. According to Dewey, self is a continuously formed through choice of action. Students become worthy individuals by education who are capable of consciously shaping their own powers and self by virtue of making choices in social realm (Dewey, 1938).

The Gita's teaching on ethics and morality are also relevant to the process of education and psychology. Dharma as prescribed and described in Gita provides an overarching framework for understanding moral duties and character of individuals. It describes the duty or Dharma of individuals in different situations of life and crisis. The focus on crisis in Gita makes it unique. A person evolves through different crises in life. Gita focuses on crisis management. Mahabharata is all about crises in life. Krishna's and other characters of Mahabharata face several emotional, psychological, personal and moral crises. Non-attachment in performing own duties is desirable and it guides a person to perform his duties without emotional burden or expectation. Selfless duty is highly emphasized in Gita. The detachment allows an individual for a selfless action without any expectation or emotional burden. It also enables the person to act selflessly, with equanimity without being influenced by any kind of negative motivations or external factors.

The relevance of Gita about ethics and morality provide a framework for understanding character and value-based education. This also relates with areas of social psychology and moral development. Any curriculum needs to develop individuals with values of honesty, responsibility, respect and empathy; essential for personal and social development. Values of compassion, peace, justice, harmony and peaceful coexistence are essential for social integration and progress in society.

The relevance of the Gita's teachings to education is not limited to the theoretical aspects only. It also provides practical guidance in educational context. in the context of teaching and learning. It has pedagogical implications. It also has practical implications for curriculum design and assessment. The concept of personalized learning is applied to Arjuna by Krishna. The principles of empathy, emotional intelligence, oneness of human race is reflected in the verse "Yo Maam Pashyati Sarvatra, Sarvam Cha mayi Pashyati; Tasyaham Na Pranashyami, Sa Cha me Na Pranashyati" (That knowledge which sees the One in all beings, and all beings in the One, is true knowledge).

Furthermore, the Gita emphasizes the importance of experiential learning and action-oriented education. Lord Krishna tells Arjuna, "Action is superior to inaction" (BG

3.8). This statement implies that learning should be connected to action and that education should aim at developing practical skills and competencies. The Gita also emphasizes the importance of self-directed learning and self-assessment, based on introspection and self-reflection. Lord Krishna tells Arjuna, "Let a man lift himself by himself. Let him not degrade himself; for the self alone is the friend of the self, and the self alone is the enemy of the self" (BG 6.5). This statement implies that education should aim at developing self-reliance and self-motivation, rather than relying on external incentives or rewards.

Furthermore, the Gita emphasizes the importance of experiential learning in life and as a pedagogy. By focusing on the importance of Karma, it establishes the prominence of doing over talking. It gives the lesson of walking the talk, learning by doing. We can see that Krishna himself says that I don't have any prescribed duties to perform but for the betterment of the world and universe, I reincarnate, engage in worldly affairs and perform my duties. The prominence of duties or Karma is pivotal in Gita. Gita also recognizes the importance of self-directed learning by mentioning at one place – Soul is the best friend of himself and best enemy also. It means a person can lift himself to the top and can be responsible for his fall at the same time.

In conclusion, the Srimad Bhagavad Gita is a valuable source of inspiration and guidance for modern education systems by providing useful insights in educational psychology, leadership and social sciences. Its teaching about self-knowledge, resolute intelligence, emotional intelligence, emotional management, anxiety and causes and resolution of anxiety; all are very valuable and intuitive theoretical frameworks with concrete implications in educational psychology. Its focus on morality and ethics provides a possible starting point for the discourse of very foundations of Indian indigenous social sciences. By integrating the Gita's teachings a more holistic and transformative system of education focused on experiential learning, decision making, problem solving and holistic living could be inculcated.

Objectives of the Study

This study aims to identify the principles of educational psychology applied in the context of Srimad Bhagavad Gita and to explain them in a coherent manner. Further it aims to design empirical procedures and psychometric measures based on the theoretical frameworks of Bhagavad Gita for the testing of their validity and reliability to some extent. It also reflects on the principles of andragogy embedded in the pious text.

CHAPTER 2
Literature Review

Studies on Educational Relevance of Religious Texts Around the World

The Bible: The Bible is the most widely studied religious text in western knowledge world. David Jefferey, in his famous book "*The bible and the University*"; argues that bible has shaped the western thought and culture broadly. As a source of literary inspiration, instruction and historical insight; it has served the western thought system as a basic framework for decades. It has a long-lasting impact on the development of liberal arts, sciences, philosophy, theology, literature and art (Jefferey, 2016)

The Quran: The Quran is the central religious text of Islam, which has influenced the knowledge disciplines of human globally across several cultures. Arab scholars have contributed significantly in advancement of medical sciences, algebra, philosophy and theology. Islamic theological framework has also influenced the scholarly knowledge disciplines. Akhtar (2008) argues that the Quran provides a comprehensive framework to understand the several cultures and how this text can inform the education in a variety of ways. According to him, it provides guidance on wide range of topics, including ethics, morality, knowledge, reason, social relations and interactions. Akhtar (2008) further highlights the importance of Quran on the development of Islamic civilization and its contribution in development of science, mathematics and philosophy

The Tao Te Ching: The Tao Te Ching is a Chinese philosophical and educational text. It has wide application for well-being, happiness and education. It has been studied across disciplines for its implications in holistic learning and integration of oposites, learning as a natural process, the power of simplicity, value of not-knowing, softness over rigidity, non-interreference, silence and reflection, focus on process, cultivation of compassion and interdependence, humble leadership in education, fluidity of knowledge and resilience through yielding. Thus this text has provided several perspectives for education and life. The text has been studied for translation and interpretation, philosophical and political applications, cultural transmission and linguistic studies, textual and linguistic analysis (Budianto, 2019; Chen, 2020; Gao, 2020; LEE, 2019; Sankheangaew, 2022; Wang, 2019; Wang, Wang, & Zolotykh, 2023). Nagel (1998) highlights that it can guide curriculum design, teaching methods, and assessment techniques.

In conclusion it can be said that these religious texts provide a rich source of knowledge, wisdom, pedagogy, and inspiration that has potential to inform educational theory and practice in modern educational systems in various ways.

Gita as a Part of Prasthantrayi

The Prasthanatrayi is a term used in Hinduism to refer to the three foundational texts of Vedanta philosophy: the Upanishads, the Bhagavad Gita, and the Brahma Sutras and it can be said that these texts have foundational impact on Indian thought and philosophy. The Upanishads, which form the final part of the Vedas, provide a philosophical interpretation of Vedic rituals and practices. They were composed between the 8th and 6th centuries BCE and explores the nature of reality, consciousness, and the self (Radhakrishnan, 1994).

Within the six core systems of Indian philosophy—commonly referred to as the Ṣaḍdarśanas—the Vedānta school undoubtedly holds a preeminent position. Revered as the pinnacle of Indian philosophical thought, it balances a profound respect for the Vedas with irrefutable logic that not only supports the Vedic worldview but also dismantles several non-Vedic ideologies. Among the world's philosophical traditions, Vedānta enjoys a unique prestige, bolstered by its reliance on the *Prasthānatraya*, the triad of fundamental texts that guide one towards the ultimate purpose of life (*prasthāna*). These works are the *Śrutiprasthāna* (Upaniṣads), the *Smṛtiprasthāna* (*Bhagwadgītā*), and the *Nyāyaprasthāna* (*Brahmasūtras*).

Of the three texts, the Upaniṣads stand supreme, being regarded as the *Śruti* or revealed scripture at the heart of Hinduism. The *Brahmasūtras* bring structure and coherence to the philosophical teachings scattered across the Upaniṣads, enabling a more systematic exploration of Vedānta's metaphysical dimensions.

Chapters in Srimad Bhagavad Gita

Chapter 1 provides the context for the dialogue. In this chapter Arjuna expresses his doubts and fears about the battle ahead and Krishna explains him the possible reasons of adherence to his duty. This chapter is named as Arjuna Vishad Yoga where questions the need for war and is hesitant to fight against his own relatives but Krishna convinces him for fighting for the just cause of Dharma.Chapter 2 begins with Lord Krishna's response to Arjuna's doubts where he explains the nature of true self and importance of detachment as Sankhya Yoga. Chapter 3 highlights the importance of performing actions without attachment and consideration of the fruits of prescribed actions according to Dharma. In Chapter 4 of or Gyana Yoga, true nature of knowledge and self-realization is discussed. Chapter 5 discusses the true nature of knowledge and sanyasa, the concept of renunciation and self. It is named as Karma Sanyasa Yoga. Chapter 6 focuses on the concept of Gyana-Vigyana Yoga, the nature of divine and demonic qualities. Chapter 8- Aksara-Parabrahman Yoga discusses the nature of divine the cycle of birth and death. Chapter 9- Raja-Vidya-Raja-Guhya Yoga focuses on importance of devotion to the divine and the nature of worldly affairs. Chapter 10, Vibhuti Yoga, emphasizes and explains the divine qualities and manifestations. Chapter 11 Visvarupa-Darsana Yoga describes the divine vision and nature of universe. Chapter 12, Bhakti Yoga describes the importance of devotion to the divine and different paths of yoga. Chapter 13, Kshetra Kshetragya Vibhag Yoga- discusses the nature of the body and the soul. Chapter 14 of Gunatraya Vibhag Yoga discusses the nature of Satva, Tamas and Rajas as three basic ingredients of personality. Chapter 15 is Purusottam Yoga which highlights the eternity of soul and nature of divine. Chapter 16, Daivasura-Sampad-Vibhaga Yoga discusses the distinction between divine (*daivī*) and demoniac (*āsurī*) traits in human nature which have implications for psychology. Chapter 17th Śraddhā-traya-vibhāga-yoga (The Yoga of Threefold Faith) discusses the nature of faith (śraddhā) which is influenced by the three gunas (Satva, Rajas and Tamas) and their impact on worship and conduct. The last and 18th chapter of Mokṣa-saṁnyāsa-yoga provides a comprehensive conclusion integrating all paths of yoga and emphasizing devotion, renunciation and Krishna's ultimate teachings.

Table 1: Chapters and Main Concepts in Srimad Bhagavad Gita

Chapter	Name	Main Concepts
1	Arjuna Vishada Yoga	Arjuna's reluctance to fight, the nature of duty
2	Sankhya Yoga	The nature of the self, the importance of detachment
3	Karma Yoga	The importance of performing one's duty without attachment
4	Jnana Yoga	The nature of knowledge and self-realization
5	Karma Sannyasa Yoga	The concept of renunciation, the nature of the self
6	Dhyana Yoga	The practice of meditation, self-discipline
7	Jnana Vijana Yoga	The nature of divine and demonic qualities
8	Aksara-Parabrahman Yoga	The nature of the divine, the cycle of birth and death
9	Raja-Vidya-Raja-Guhya Yoga	The importance of devotion to the divine, the nature of the world
10	Vibhuti Yoga	The divine qualities and manifestations

Chapter	Name	Main Concepts
11	Visvarupa-Darsana Yoga	The divine vision, the nature of the universe
12	Bhakti Yoga	The importance of devotion to the divine, different paths of yoga
13	Ksetra-Ksetrajna Vibhaga Yoga	The nature of the body and the soul
14	Gunatraya-Vibhaga Yoga	The three qualities of nature: sattva, rajas, and tamas
15	Purusottama Yoga	The nature of the divine, the eternal tree of life
16	Daivasura-Sampad-Vibhaga Yoga	The divine and demonic qualities and behaviors
17	Sraddhatraya-Vibhaga Yoga	The importance of faith in spiritual practice
18	Moksha-Sannyasa Yoga	The summary of the teachings, the importance of fulfilling one's duty without attachment

Bibliometric Overview of Research on Srimad Bhagavad Gita

To have an overview of the impact of bible in scholarly publications around the world, a bibliometric search was performed on Dimensions database which resulted into 55,909 publications including 36,668 articles, 15,745 chapters, 1897 monographs, 1013 edited books, 399 preprints and 187 proceedings overall (Table 2). This wider impact gives a general overview of impact of bible on scholarly publications. This overview will help us in situating how Srimad Bhagavad Gita has influenced scholarly publications world-wide. Although it is based on *Dimensions* database which is representative of one of the most scientific databases.

Table 2: Type of Publication on Srimad Bhagavad Gita

PUBLICATION TYPE	
❍ **Article**	36,668
❍ **Chapter**	15,745
❍ **Monograph**	1,897
❍ **Edited Book**	1,013
❍ **Preprint**	399
❍ **Processing**	187

Dimensions database on a search of the keyword Quran, provides that 18779 articles have been published about impact of Quran in different disciplines. This provides a snapshot of scholarly impact of the religious text. Although printed and non-indexed publications can be much more than this figure.

The Bhagavad Gita

The Bhagavad Gita has been studied widely for its educational, religious, social, cultural and psychological relevance by several scholars. Mishra (2024) argues that the Gita provides a comprehensive practical view for understanding educational and social interactions as well it provides feasible solutions in terms of concrete actions.

A bibliometric Review of Studies on Gita

A brief bibliometric analysis based on thee Scopus database was conducted for an overview of publications on Gita in academic world. It provides a snapshot of how Gita has influenced academic discourse and guided several industrial and social problems through its practical potential.

Table 3: Overview of Publications on Srimad Bhagavad Gita

Category	Description
MAIN INFORMATION ABOUT DATA	
Timespan	1933:2025
Sources (Journals, Books, etc)	314
Documents	455
Annual Growth Rate %	0
Document Average Age	9.23
Average citations per doc	4.532
References	16505
DOCUMENT CONTENTS	
Keywords Plus (ID)	438
Author's Keywords (DE)	1080
AUTHORS	
Authors	588
Authors of single-authored docs	278
AUTHORS COLLABORATION	
Single-authored docs	319
Co-Authors per Doc	1.57

Category	Description
International co-authorships %	5.495
DOCUMENT TYPES	
Article	232
Book	33
Book Chapter	129
Conference Paper	19
Review	42

As presented in Table 3, the bibliometric analysis of **Srimad Bhagavad Gita** publications (1933–2025) includes 455 documents from 314 sources, with a steady growth rate and an average document age of 9.23 years. Research spans articles (232), books (33), chapters (129), reviews (42), and conference papers (19), averaging 4.532 citations per document. Contributions come from 588 authors, with 319 single-authored works and 5.5% international collaboration. Keywords Plus (438) and Author Keywords (1,080) reflect diverse themes, showing consistent academic interest across disciplines.

Publications on the Bhagavad Gita began with 1 article in 1933 and remained sparse until 1980 (peaking at 3 articles). The number grew steadily post-2000 (e.g., 5 articles in 2004, 30 in 2016), and peaked at 52 articles in 2023. It could be observed that the growth in publications accelerated after 2000, with averaging 5 articles in 2004, 9 in 2006, 21 in 2010 and 30 in 2016. In recent consistent high outputs, including 35 articles in 2022, peaking at 52 in 2023, with 29 projected for 2024 could be observed.

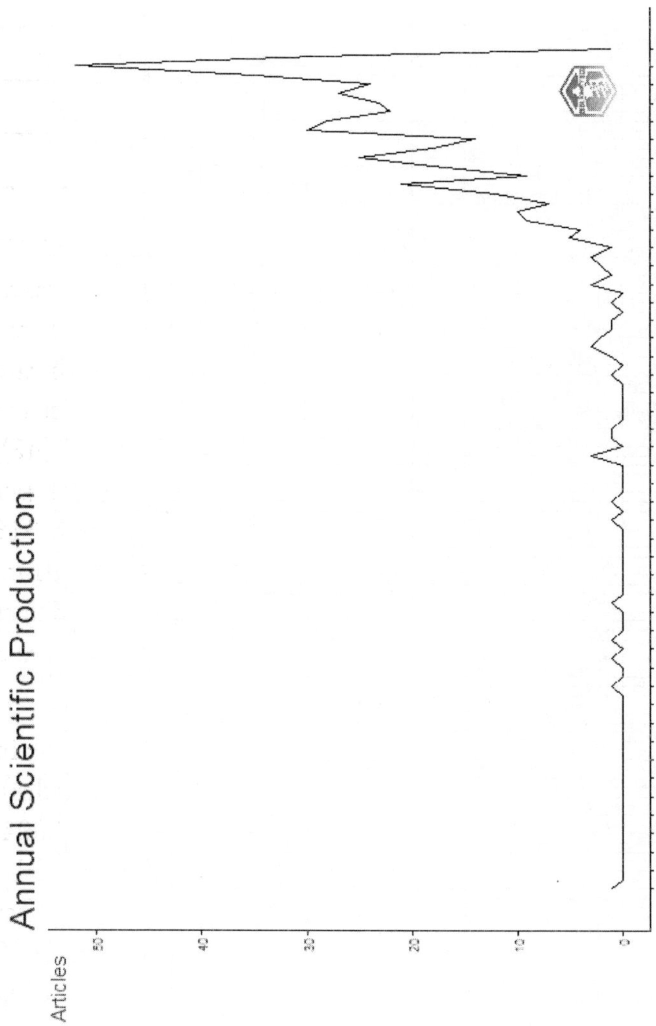

Figure 1: Annual Scientific Production of Research on Gita

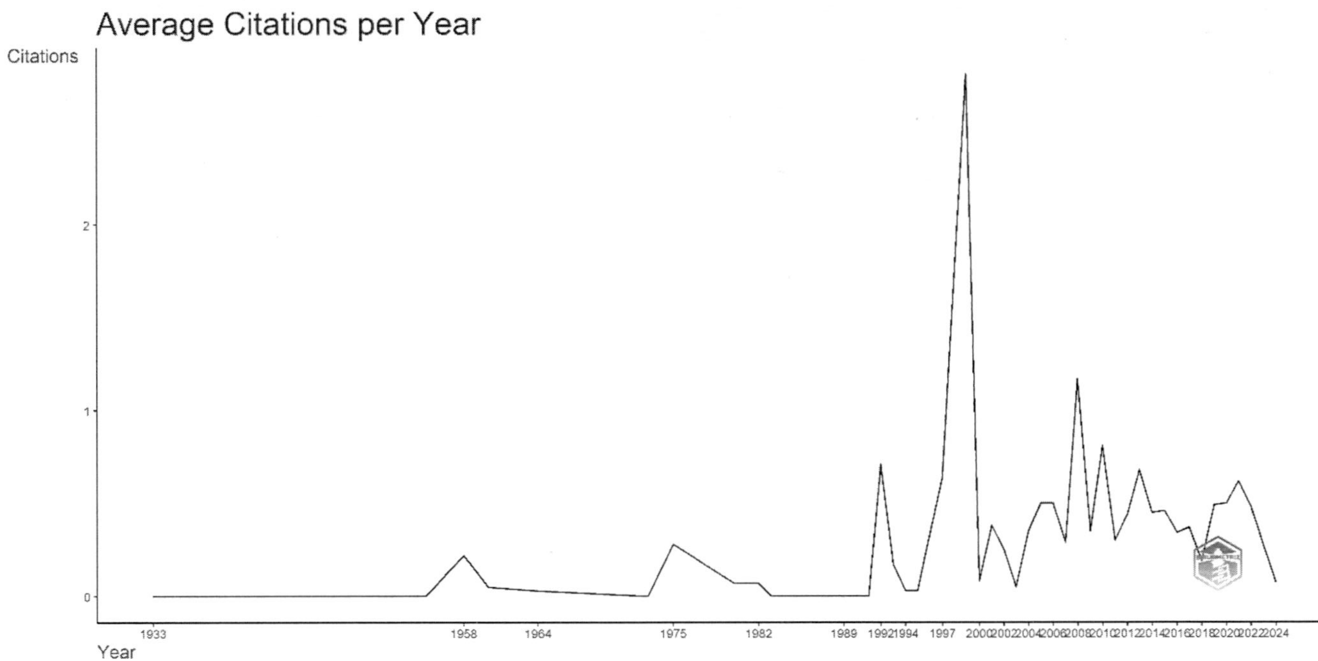

Figure 2: Average Citations Per Year on Srimad Bhagavad Gita

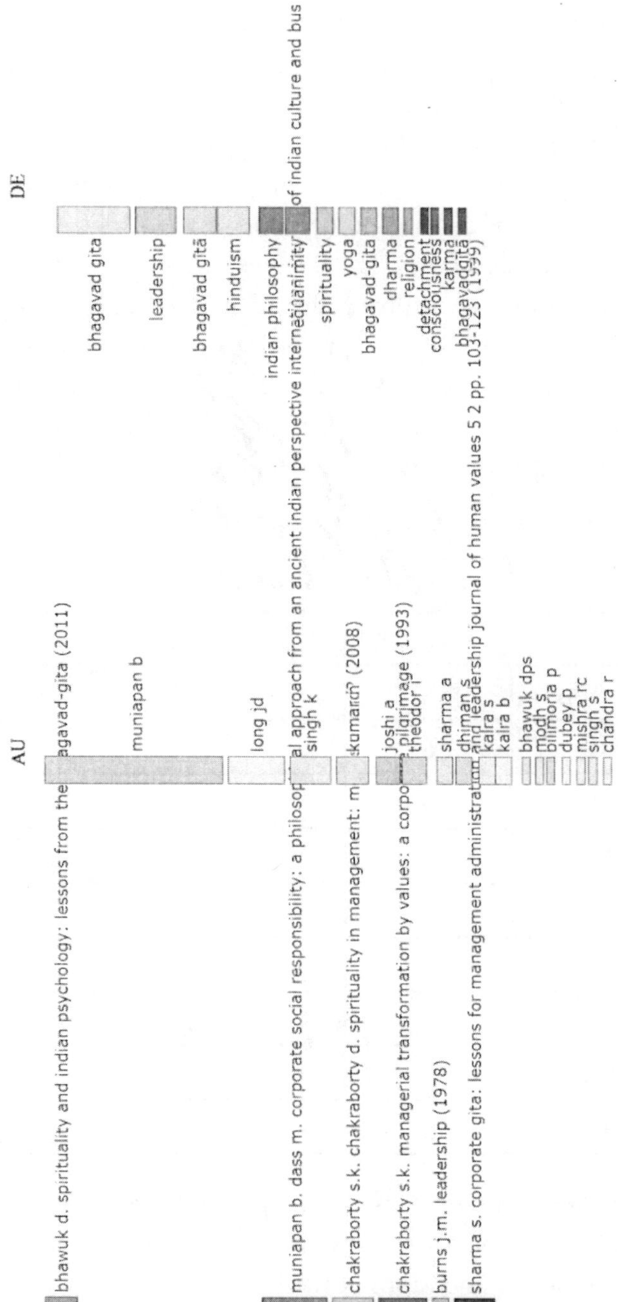

Figure 3: Sanky Diagram

The Sankey diagram connects Cited References (CR), Authors (AU), and Keywords (DE) in global research focused on Bhagavad. Key references include works by Bhawuk D. (spirituality and psychology), Muniapan B. (corporate social responsibility), and Chakraborty S. K. (spirituality in management). Influential authors, such as Muniapan B., Sharma A., and Chakraborty D., have explored themes like leadership, Hinduism, and spirituality which indicates about the core relevance of Gita. Prominent keywords include Bhagavad Gita, leadership, spirituality, yoga, dharma, and management. It reflects a focus on applying Gita's teachings in philosophy, management, and self-awareness.

Table 4: Key Contributors to Bhagavad Gita Research

Authors	Articles	Articles Fractionalized
JOSHI A	6	1.24
MUNIAPAN B	6	5
THEODOR I	6	6
BILIMORIA P	5	5
DHIMAN S	5	5
KUMAR N	5	2.67
SINGH K	4	1.58
SINGH S	4	2.17
STROUD SR	4	4
BHAWUK DPS	3	3

Table 4: Key contributors to Bhagavad Gita Research based on dimensions database. Key contributors to Bhagavad Gita research include Theodor I contributing 6 articles which are all independently authored., Muniapan B contributes

6 articles with a strong individual focus on corporate responsibility. Bilimoria P and Dhiman S contributed 5 articles each, emphasizing leadership and spirituality. Joshi A has 6 articles with a highly collaborative teamwork and Kumar N (5 articles, moderately collaborative) reflect teamwork in their research. Singh K, Singh S, Stroud SR, and Bhawuk DPS contribute 3–4 articles each exploring diverse themes. Bhawuk focusing on Indian psychology and spirituality. These authors highlight the Gita's relevance across philosophy, leadership, and management.

Table 5: Countries Scientific Production

Countries Scientific Production Region	Frequency
INDIA	355
USA	143
UK	38
AUSTRALIA	26
CANADA	12
MALAYSIA	9
SOUTH AFRICA	8
ISRAEL	7
KAZAKHSTAN	5
BANGLADESH	4

India leads with 355 publications on Gita worldwide. USA is the second country with 143 publications. UK and Australia with 38 and 26 publications acquire third and fourth places. Other countries are Canada, Malayasia, South Africa, Israel, Kazakhstan and Bangladesh.

Thematic Map

The factorial thematic diagram generated by Biblioshiny (R) software provides an overview of academic research influenced by Gita. Mental health and stress management have been among the most frequent and applied issues in Gita. Its importance also raised in COVID-19 pandemic. Ethical leadership in industrial and management is also studied from the perspective of Gita.

Meditation, awareness, mindfulness and cultural heritage could be seen. Its connection with Hindu tradition and culture could be seen in the researched themes. Gita has been studied in the field of artificial intelligence and computational linguistics for its possible use in language processing and ethical decision making.

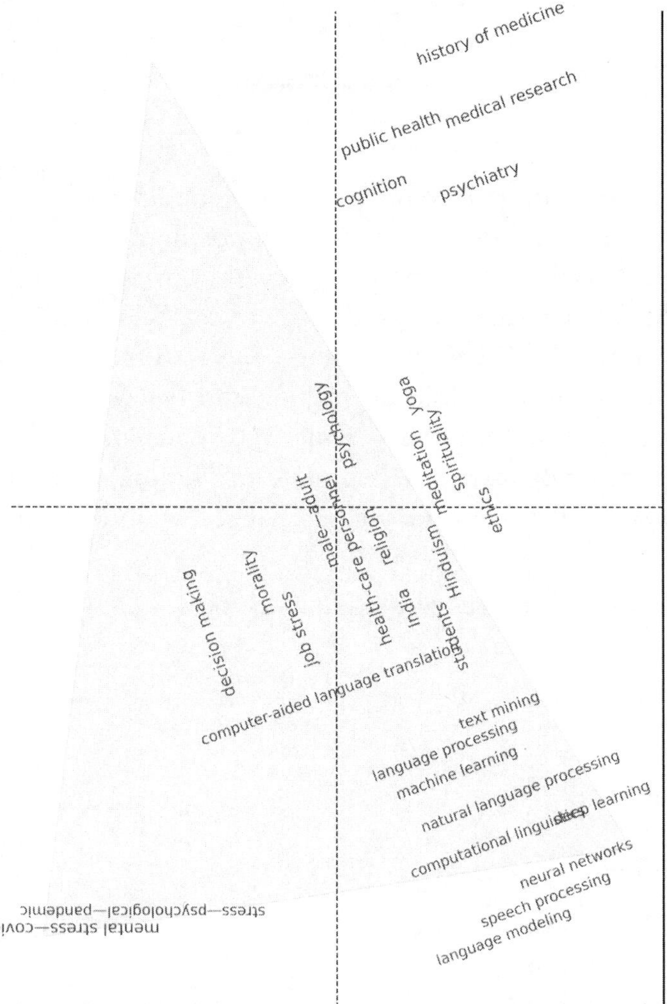

Figure 4: Thematic Map of Bhagavad Gita Research.

CHAPTER 3
Methodology

Educational psychology as an interdisciplinary field focuses on understanding and improving the behavior of student, teaching-learning process, and learning outcomes. It applies the principles of psychology to the field of education for addressing issues of learning, motivation, adjustment, conflict-resolution, decision making and behavioral change. In this context Gita offers significant discussion on human mind, consciousness, ego, behavior, meditation, mindfulness, decision-making and behavioral change. As an ancient text,

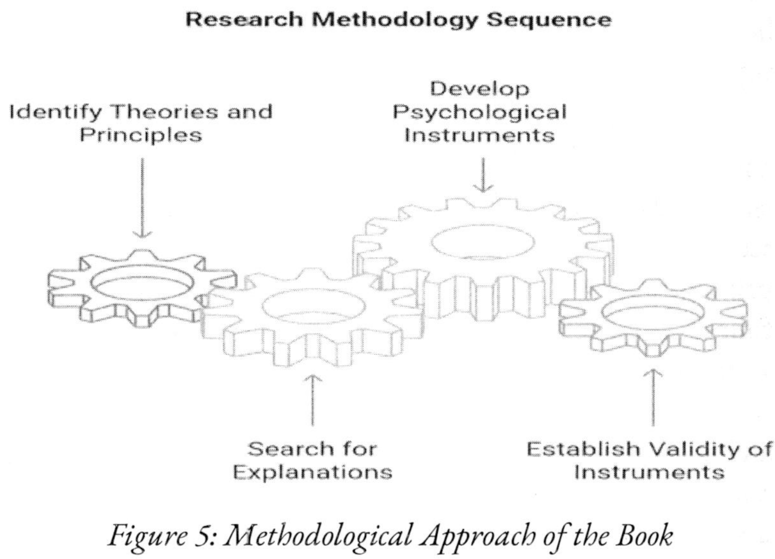

Figure 5: Methodological Approach of the Book

it offers unique psychological perspectives rooted in cultural insights and heritage, which is timeless and relevant to modern-day challenges.

The first step of the research was to identify the theories and principles embedded in the Srimad Bhagavad Gita. By taking parallels to the modern psychological texts and comparing and juxta-positioning them with the principles and theories stated in Srimad Bhagavad Gita, this study aims to explore those parallels and unique insights which are rooted indigenously in Indian culture. Authentic commentaries and their translations are used to analyze the text. This step also used empirical insights from qualitative and quantitative research literature.

After identifying the theories of educational psychology in Gita, the next step was to search for the possible explanation for these theories. The theories are deductively derived from Gita and offer a unique explanation in Indian context and has the potential for universal application. The process of identifying and explaining these concepts and theories helped in developing a theoretical framework of educational psychology which is integrative and comprehensive.

The next step involved development of psychological scales and identification of dimensions of emotional intelligence, leadership, resolute intelligence, and life satisfaction. This section helps in understanding the practical use of these principles. Based on expert opinion these tools provide a foundational work of psychometric assessment based on spiritual practices from Gita. These instruments are designed to measure specific aspects of life satisfaction, leadership, and intelligence. Further, this discussion provides insights about psychological processes identified in the text. These instruments were validated by experts' opinions.

In conclusion, the study highlights the relevance and importance of Srimad Bhagavad Gita in the field of educational psychology. The study uses deducto-inductive method of inquiry for identifying the principles, assumptions and theories of psychology in Gita. After identifying these theories, their explanations are offered and interpreted. Some important concepts, such as life satisfaction and leadership, are used to develop instruments. Thus, it offers a theoretical framework, overview of psychological concepts useful in education and develops some foundational psychological instruments based on Gita.

Chapter 4

Principles of Educational Psychology Applied in the Context of Srimad Bhagavad Gita

There are numerous psychological principles embedded in Srimad Bhagavad Gita.

Table no 6 explains the psychological principles present and relevant shlokas.

Table 6: Psychological Principle, Chapter and Shloka Numbers

Psychological Principle	Chapter and Shloka Numbers
Emotional Intelligence	Chapter 2, Shlokas 54-72; Chapter 6, Shlokas 26-30
Mindfulness	Chapter 6, Shlokas 10-15; Chapter 12, Shloka 1
Self-awareness	Chapter 3, Shloka 42; Chapter 4, Shlokas 34-35
Self-regulation	Chapter 3, Shlokas 36-43; Chapter 6, Shlokas 23-24

Psychological Principle	Chapter and Shloka Numbers
Resilience	Chapter 2, Shloka 14; Chapter 12, Shlokas 6-7
Perseverance	Chapter 2, Shloka 47; Chapter 6, Shlokas 24-25
Compassion	Chapter 13, Shloka 29; Chapter 14, Shloka 16
Authenticity	Chapter 3, Shloka 35; Chapter 4, Shlokas 38-39; Chapter 18, Shloka 47
Transcendence	Chapter 2, Shloka 45; Chapter 5, Shlokas 24-26
Self-transformation	Chapter 2, Shlokas 11-30; Chapter 3, Shlokas 3-9
Ego transcendence	Chapter 3, Shlokas 19-20; Chapter 5, Shloka 7; Chapter 18, Shlokas 53-54
Mind-body connection	Chapter 5, Shlokas 27-28; Chapter 6, Shlokas 12-15
Self-compassion	Chapter 6, Shloka 32; Chapter 12, Shloka 13
Forgiveness	Chapter 11, Shloka 33; Chapter 16, Shloka 3
Self-acceptance	Chapter 18, Shloka 66
Non-judgmental awareness	Chapter 2, Shloka 47; Chapter 12, Shloka 1

Psychological Principle	Chapter and Shloka Numbers
Interconnectedness	Chapter 13, Shlokas 28-29; Chapter 18, Shloka 63
Graciousness	Chapter 2, Shloka 5; Chapter 12, Shloka 14
Mind-body integration	Chapter 6, Shloka 10; Chapter 12, Shloka 1
Self-transcendence	Chapter 2, Shloka 45; Chapter 5, Shlokas 24-26
Freedom from attachment	Chapter 2, Shlokas 62-63; Chapter 3, Shlokas 34-35
Self-reflection	Chapter 3, Shloka 40; Chapter 6, Shloka 20

The table provides a summary of the main psychological principles discussed in the Srimad Bhagavad Gita, along with the relevant chapter and shloka numbers.

Emotional Intelligence

The concept of emotional intelligence is imbedded in mainly chapter 2 and chapter 6. Chapter 2 (Shloka 54-72) and Chapter 6 (Shloka 26-30). Gita constantly emphasizes the control of mind over senses. Surprisingly the metaphor of chariot of senses and charioteer of mind is used by Plato also. Controlling senses through a disciplined and focused mind is emphasized in Gita.

Mindfulness

Mindfulness is mentioned in chapter 6 (Shlokas 10-15), and Chapter 12 (Shloka 1). Mindfulness is considered to maintain a psychological awareness about one's thoughts emotions, and actions. Mindfulness helps in controlling the mind and one's emotions.

Self-awareness

Self-awareness and mindfulness are related concepts. The importance of self-awareness is mentioned in Chapter 3 (Shloka 42) and Chapter 4 (Shlokas 34-35). Understanding one's thoughts, cognitive process, emotions, actions is an important aspect of yoga an balanced life. For a yogi, self-awareness is one important practice and guideline. The main purpose of self-awareness lies in making conscious choices and taking responsibility of your actions.

Self-regulation

Self-regulation is emphasized in Chapter 3 (Shlokas 36-43) and Chapter 6 (Shloka 23-24). The practice of self-regulation is emphasized by Gita which involves self control. Self-control of thoughts, emotions and actions. Complete cognitive, affective and motor control is emphasized in Gita. Without self-regulation one can't exercise his choices rationally and can't overcome negative emotions and desires which lead to inner peace and harmony.

Positive Psychology

Chapter 2 (Shlokas 40-48) and Chapter 12 (Shloka 13) provide some instances of positive psychology dealing with the concept of optimism, hope and faith. These frameworks can help individuals cope with stress and challenge in situations of crises.

Resilience : Chapter 2 (Shloka 14) and Chapter 12 (Shloka 6-7) emphasize the importance of resilience. It is the ability to make a come back from setbacks and challenges and requires inner strength and determination to survive and grow.

Perseverance

Chapter 2 (Shloka 47) and Chapter 6 (Shlokas 24-25) highlight the importance of perseverance as a psychological process. Focus on task, consistency and selfless effort are key to perseverance. Perseverance is correlated with academic success and other positively considered behavioral outcomes. It helps in achieving one's goals despite challenges and obstacles.

Gratitude

Chapter 7 (Shloka 11-12) and Chapter 9 (Shloka 26-27) are central to this concept. Gratitude is one of the core values in Indian moral theory and philosophy. Ungratefulness is seen as a vice. Gratefulness includes acknowledgement and appreciation of the blessings or help of others in life. Gratefulness can help in fostering a positive mindset and gesture and can help in overcoming anxiety.

Compassion

Chapter 13 (Shloka 29) and Chapter 14 (Shloka 16) emphasize the need of understanding and empathizing with others. Compassionate teachers can understand the feelings and emotions of students. This can help in reducing anxiety and emotional burnout in student. It is also useful in developing positive relationships and reducing conflicts between teacher and students.

Authenticity

Authenticity is described in Chapter 3 (Shloka 35), Chapter 4 (Shloka 38-39) and Chapter 18 (Shloka 47). Aligning oneself to own true nature, self and values is authenticity. No difference between thoughts and deeds is needed to achieve this. Authenticity has been studied in educational research in language education (Jacobs, Asmawi, & Renandya, 2022), science education (Anker-Hansen & Andreé, 2019), social justice (Bialystok & Kukar, 2017), biology education (Yarden & Carvalho, 2011), modeling in science education (Schriebl, Müller, & Robin, 2022), spirituality in higher education (Chickering, 2006), project-based learning (Svensson, Adawi, & Johansson, 2021), and brand management in higher education institutions (Girardin, Blal, & Lunardo, 2023).

Transcendence

Chapter 2 (Shloka 45) and Chapter 5 (Shlokas 24-26) discuss the concept of transcendence of ego to understand the true nature of self and atman. It is also imperative for understanding the equality and connection of all souls with God. Karma and Yoga are major methods of transcending the ego. By practicing yoga one can transcend the material world and connect with divine.

Self-transformation

Reaching higher level of consciousness is emphasized in Gita. Chapter 2 (Shlokas 11-30) and Chapter 3 (Shlokas 3-9) emphasize self-transformation. Transformation of self to reach a higher level of understanding about oneself and universe can be achieved only by practicing righteous Karma and Yoga. Chapter 3 emphasize the need of righteous and selfless karma for achieving the state of pure mind and self-transformation.

Mind-body Connection

Chapter 5 (Shlokas 27-28) and Chapter 6 (Shlokas 12-15) highlight the importance of mind-body connection for achieving spiritual growth in life. Spirituality is the true nature of human being and its full development is one of the highest goals of life in Gita. Goals help in living a purposeful life. Purposelessness can be seen as a lost sense of meaning and purpose in one's life. Chapter 5, Shloka 27 suggests for controlling the senses by mind to achieve peace and tranquility in life. Control of senses by mind is a central theme in Gita and several metaphors are used to explain and elaborate it. Practicing Yoga can help achieve control over the mind and body (Chapter 6, Shlokas 12-15).

Self-compassion

Chapter 6 (Shloka 32) and Chapter 12 (Shloka 13) provide a deep meaning and importance of self-compassion in achieving peace and tranquility. The highest Yogi understands the ability to see oneself in others and others in oneself by the virtue of likeness of the self. Only a self-compassionate person can recognize their own experiences of pain and pleasure and understand the pain and suffering of others. The self-compassion is a mean to the end of broader connection with other souls and ultimate being. Similarly, Chapter 12 (Shloka 13) emphasizes the importance of recognition of oneness, emotional equanimity, action without ego and mindful forgiveness as needed practices for self-compassion to achieve enlightenment.

Forgiveness

Chapter 11 (Shloka 33) and Chapter 16 (Shloka 2) emphasize the need of forgiveness for living a peaceful life. It is seen as a strength and not a weakness. Karma and human fallibility provie a basis of empathy which is rooted in understanding. Forgiveness is also considered a form of liberation which frees us from cycle of resentment fostering spiritual growth and inner peace. It breaks the cycle of vengeance, recognizes the shared human fallibility. Being forgiving is being divine. It works as emotional closure of rebirth and emotional accumulation of karmas. It is essential to achieve growth.

Self-acceptance: Chapter 18 (Shloka 66) describes the need of self-acceptance. Self-acceptance is necessary for accepting one's true nature as divine and accepting the prescribed duties of Dharma and performing it without any attachment and expectation of results. Krishna argues for acceptance of your true being as a part of ultimate being and by virtue of understanding true self one can surrender himself or herself to the God. This self-acceptance resolves several crisis and conflicts of person in order to achieve enlightenment.

Graciousness

In Chapter 2 (Shloka 5) and Chapter 12 (Shloka 14) Gita reflects the need of graciousness in an enlightened individual. Performing one's duties without any attachment and with evenness, gracious decision making, empathy in conflict and preferring inner integrity over outer success is prioritized. It is reflected in kindness and empathy toward others, balanced emotional response, humility, forgiveness, contentment and self-control. In Chapter 12, Shloka 14, Krishna states that those who are gracious, self-content, devoted, self-controlled, faithful, have surrendered their ego; and kind-hearted are dear to him.

Freedom from Attachment

Chapter 2 (Shlokas 62-63) are focused on freedom from attachment. Constant contemplation of sensory objects creates attachment which creates desire. Nonavailability or unmet desire produces anger. Anger clouds the rational judgement which causes loss of memory leading to destruction of intellect and ruination. Mind has a natural tendency towards external objects of pleasure. Unchecked desire becomes insatiable and anger is its byproduct. In condition of anger, memory is clouded and person forgets all the previous experiences and information about right decision.

Self-reflection

Chapter 3 (Shloka 40) emphasizes the importance of self-reflection. Self-reflection has implications for regulating the senses, disciplining the mind, strengthening the intellect and redirecting desires towards just causes. Senses are primary interface with outer world. The mind consolidates data and magnifies attachment into strong desires. The intellect provides judgment but can be swayed away by strong emotions or desires. Only the knowledge of true self can help in navigating life meaningfully.

It can be said that Srimad Bhagavad Gita includes several psychological concepts of educational implications such as Emotional Intelligence, Mindfulness, Self-awareness, Self-regulation, Resilience, Perseverance, Compassion, Authenticity, Transcendence, Self-transformation, Ego transcendence, Mind-body connection, Self-compassion, Forgiveness, Self-acceptance, Non-judgmental awareness, Interconnectedness, Graciousness, Mind-body integration, Self-transcendence, Freedom from attachment and Self-reflection. It offers valuable insights, whether read as a spiritual text, a philosophical treatise, or a guide.

CHAPTER 5

Explaining Concepts of Educational Psychology Present in Gita

Emotional Intelligence in Srimad Bhagavad Gita

Emotional Intelligence (EI) has gained attention in academic circles since Salovey & Mayer (1990) have proposed this construct. Goleman (1995) popularized emotional intelligence which further fueled the research in this area of psychology. Emotional Intelligence can be defined as the ability to recognize, understand and manage emotions. It is also the ability to understand the emotions of others in order to guide thought and behavior in a unique manner. In this section, a brief overview of theoretical backgrounds of emotional intelligence is presented and then an analysis of emotional intelligence in the context of Gita is presented.

Theoretical Framework of Emotional Intelligence

Salovey and Mayer (1990) introduced the concept of emotional intelligence with a four-dimensional construct consisting of the ability to perceive emotions accurately, using emotions to facilitate thinking, to understand the imbedded meaning in emotional content and to manage emotions effectively. Later, Daniel Golman (2005) popularized it and proposed 5 dimensions in the construct. These included self-awareness, self-regulation, motivation, empathy and social skills. The concept has been widely researched and modified by several scholars proposing several theoretical frameworks to understand emotional intelligence. The ability model, the mixed model and the trait model are main theoretical frameworks to understand the concept of emotional intelligence (Petrides, 2011).

The Ability Model of Emotional Intelligence

The ability model of emotional intelligence proposes that emotional intelligence is a set of cognitive abilities required to perceive, understand and regulate own and others emotions (Mayer, Salovey, & Caruso, 2000). It can be described as an ability to reason about emotions and use emotional information to enhance thought. It includes perceiving emotions, using emotions to facilitate thought, understanding emotions and managing thoughts. Emotional intelligence can be defined as a mental ability and should be assessed on ability based measurement as a best choice. Intelligence and behavior may differ and although it predict tendencies but does not guarantee specific behaviors which may be influenced by personality and social context. Although revisions have been made by the authors, and new problem-solving abilities have been proposed to be added in the model; such as recognizing cultural variations in emotions and forecasting emotional outcomes. It was found that the use of emotions lacked strong psychometric evidence as a distinct ability but remains conceptually relevant.

The Mixed Model of Emotional Intelligence

The mixed model of emotional intelligence is based on the assumption that emotional intelligence is composed of mental abilities and personality traits and competencies. Golman (1998) model includes self-awareness, self-regulation, motivation, empathy, and social skills. Bar-On (2004) proposes that emotional intelligence is composed of interpersonal skills, intrapersonal skills, adaptability, stress management and General mood. Although measurement of mixed model-based tests is criticized upon the fact that these overlap with the ability models.

The Trait Model of Emotional Intelligence

The trait model of emotional intelligence proposes that emotional intelligence is a constellation of self-perceptions about emotional abilities which are grounded in personality theories (Petrides & Furnham, 2000). This model operates outside the cognitive ability framework and aligns with big five personality traits. Traits models are criticised for blurring the boundaries between personality traits and emotional intelligence. It relates emotional intelligence with personality traits such as extraversion and neurociticism.

Emotional Intelligence in Srimad Bhagavad Gita is explained in chapter 2 in form of self-awareness and control (Chapter 2, Shloka 55-57), Mood Management (Shloka 62-63), Detachment (Shloka 47-49), Equanimity (Shloka 38), Peace and Liberation (Shloka 65 and 71). The table provides a comprehensive overview of principles embedded in the Gita. Shloka 58 compares a self-aware person to a tortoise withdrawing its limbs which signifies self-control over sensory inputs. Self-restrain and control are central themes within the emotional management framework of Gita. An individual who masters his senses through yoga and Samyak karma, achieves the perfect knowledge (Chapter 2, Shloka 68). Similarly, Shloka 69 describes the importance of self-awareness as an awakened being.

Mood management is also a central theme in Gita. Chapter 2 (Shloka 59) explains why the taste for sensory pleasures diminishes in awakened persons. While shlokas 62 and 63 warn about the attachment that leads to desires and unfulfilled desires result in anger, delusion and destruction of self. Peace and clarity are fruits of mastering emotional disturbances and senses (Shloka 65).

Social awareness of the environment and societal context is a prerequisite of emotional stability. In chapter 2, Shloka 55 describes a wise person who gives up all desires and finds contentment within himself. Similarly, shloka 56 emphasizes freedom from attachment, fear, and anger for achieving emotional stability. Shlokas 60 and 61 highlight the challenges of sensory control and prescribe the Karma Yoga for ordinary people and Gyan Yoga for scholars.

Relationship Management

The need for maintaining stable relationships is vital in society. Chapter 2 (Shloka 57) emphasizes detachment from both good and bad and remaining emotionally stable in all relationships. Maintaining emotional balance is required for stable relationship. Similalry, Shloka 66 suggests that an undisciplined mind creates illusion and impacts interpersonal relations negatively. Shloka 70 uses the analogy of an ocean unaffected by rivers, reflects the need for emotional stability in emotional exchanges.

Control of Senses

Gita emphasizes need for mastery over sensory inputs and temptations to prevent emotional disturbances. Shloka 58 (Chapter 2) compares a sensible person as a tortoise who withdraws his limbs into his shell. Alike a tortoise, a controlled and self-restrained person withdraws his attention from subjects of sensual pleasures. Uncontrolled senses are a source of emotional turmoil, and mastery over senses is essential for emotional stability. It could be achieved through disciplined practice of Karma or righteous action.

Control of Desires

Managing cravings and desires is necessary for attaining detachment. Withdrawal of senses from their subjects is one of the needed strategies in Gita for emotional stability. Apart from this Shloka 55 renunciates that a person who has given up desires achieves peace. Moreover, Shloka 62 explains how attachment to desires leads to anger an emotional instability. Shloka 39 (Chapter 3) identifies desire as the root cause of emotional disturbance.

Control of Anger (Krodha), Detachment (Anasakti) and Emotional Stability (Sthitpragyata)

Shloka 63 (Chapter 2), explains anger as a cause of delusion, memory loss and destruction of intellect. Anger arises from unfulfilled desires and expectations due to previous attachment with the subject of senses and pleasures. Krishna emphasizes understanding the origin of desires and developing self-control to prevent emotional and intellectual damage (Chapter 3, 41). Detachment or (Anasakti) is about practicing non-attachment to the results of actions to maintain emotional balance in the individual. Shlokas 47-49 (Chapter 2) advocate for performing duties without attachment to the outcome and detachment from the material desires leads to peace and tranquillity (Shloka 71, Chapter 2). Equanimity in pleasure and pain leads to a stable mind which include freedom from fear, anger and desires. Thus, Gita necessitates emotional regulation by practicing detachment, controlling anger and desires to achieve inner peace and liberation.

Table 7 : Psychological Concepts in Srimad Bhagavad Gita

Principle	Description	Source (Bhagavad-Gita Shloka)	Insights/Comments	References
Self-Awareness	Awareness of one's emotions, strengths, weaknesses, and inner self.	2:58, 2:68, 2:69	Described as "Stithapragya" or stabilized wisdom. Withdraws senses like a tortoise, unaffected by external stimuli.	Gayathri & Meenakshi (2012), Mahimna Vyas (2018), Sivakumar (2021).
Mood Management	Control over emotions such as anger, fear, and sorrow to maintain balance and positivity.	2:59, 2:62-63, 2:65	Anger clouds judgment; control achieved through discipline and divine focus.	Gayathri & Meenakshi (2012), Sivakumar (2021).
Social Awareness	Awareness of one's social surroundings and ability to express and manage emotions appropriately.	2:55, 2:56, 2:61	Includes overcoming attachment and aversion; fostering empathy and connectedness.	Sivakumar (2021), Gayathri & Meenakshi (2012).

Principle	Description	Source (Bhagavad-Gita Shloka)	Insights/Comments	References
Relationship Management	Building and sustaining healthy relationships through understanding and emotional balance.	2:57, 2:64-66, 2:70	Described using the metaphor of an ocean remaining undisturbed by rivers; detachment from material desires is key.	Mahimna Vyas (2018), Sivakumar (2021).
Control of Senses	Purification and mastery over sensory inputs to maintain emotional stability.	2:58, 3:41, 14:18	Progression from tamas (ignorance) to rajas (activity) to sattva (knowledge). Achieved through discipline and detachment.	Sivakumar (2021), Gayathri & Meenakshi (2012).
Control of Desires (Kama)	Managing desires to avoid attachment and dissatisfaction, focusing only on ethical and righteous desires.	2:55, 2:62, 3:39	Negative desires hinder emotional stability; control leads to tranquility.	Sivakumar (2021), Mahimna Vyas (2018).

Principle	Description	Source (Bhagavad-Gita Shloka)	Insights/Comments	References
Control of Anger (Krodha)	Recognizing anger as a result of unfulfilled desires and preventing its destructive consequences.	2:63	Anger leads to delusion, memory loss, and destruction of intellect; managing desires helps in anger control.	Sivakumar (2021), Gayathri & Meenakshi (2012).
Detachment (Anasakti)	Non-attachment to outcomes of actions, leading to peace and emotional balance.	2:47-49, 2:71	Concept of "Karma Yoga" - focus on duty without attachment to results.	Gayathri & Meenakshi (2012), Sivakumar (2021), Mahimna Vyas (2018).
Emotional Stability (Sthitapragya)	The state of emotional stability and wisdom, unaffected by external dualities such as pleasure and pain.	2:15, 2:55-57	Emotional stability leads to peace, liberation, and higher knowledge.	Sivakumar (2021), Gayathri & Meenakshi (2012).

Principle	Description	Source (Bhagavad-Gita Shloka)	Insights/Comments	References
Mind Management (Manas)	Controlling the fickle mind to prevent oscillations between attachment and aversion, ensuring tranquility and clarity.	2:64, 6:35	Achieved through "Vairagya" (detachment) and repeated practice ("Abhyasa").	Sivakumar (2021), Mahimna Vyas (2018).
Balance in Dualities	Maintaining equanimity in success and failure, gain and loss, pleasure and pain.	2:38	A key tenet of emotional intelligence; crucial for decision-making and emotional balance.	Gayathri & Meenakshi (2012), Sivakumar (2021).
Liberation through Emotional Regulation	Emotional regulation leads to liberation and transcendence, as material desires and dualities no longer affect the individual.	2:15, 2:71, 2:52	Liberation arises from detachment and emotional stability; aligns with modern EI's goal of achieving personal and professional success.	Gayathri & Meenakshi (2012), Sivakumar (2021).

CHAPTER 6
Mindfulness

Research on Mindfulness indicates that it is a trending topic due to its applied nature in academic and industrial contexts. As enhanced attention and moment-by-moment awareness, it involves a heightened state of involvement and wakefulness. It also advocates for being in the present and maintaining an open and non-judgmental consciousness. There are normally two views presented as the definition of mindfulness in research. One is about trait mindfulness, which is related to the biological characteristics of a stable disposition and enduring personality aspect that can be enhanced or maintained through practices.

The further state of mindfulness is defined as a purposeful attention, which occurs only while an individual intentionally focuses their attention on the practice of mindfulness. State mindfulness is sustained through intentional effort. (Bishop et al., 2004) have provided two-component definition of state mindfulness. First is self-regulation of attention and second is maintaining curiosity and openness to whatever arises in the present moment. Kabat-Zinn (2013) developed a program, MBSR (Mindfulness-Based Stress Reduction) which aimed to help individuals in managing chronic pain and stress. This program popularized its use and fueled further research in this area.

Ancient Buddhists practiced mindfulness as a medium to develop awareness and insight into the present moment. Recently, western psychologists have adopted the concept and practice of mindfulness. Mindfulness-based Interventions (MBIs) include a variety of programs, such as MBSR, MBCT, MBRP. These programs have shown effectiveness in treatment of mental health conditions (Khoury et al., 2015). Brown and Ryan (2003) found empirical evidence for linking mindfulness to self-regulation and well-being of the individual. Baer (2003) conducted a review of mindfulness interventions for their conceptual and empirical structures. Shapiro et al. provide a foundational theoretical framework for understanding mindfulness. They have also worked on explaining mechanisms of action by which mindfulness influences other aspects of a personality. Their model of mindfulness has three components—intention, attention and attitude. Intention is the motivation behind practice, attention is focused, sustained and flexible awareness of moment, and attitude is the quality of attention marked by kindness, curiosity and acceptance (Kabat-Zinn, 1990; Bishop et al., 2004).

Mindfulness in Gita

Knowingly or unknowingly, the modern concept of mindfulness has significantly borrowed from the Gita. Especially in Chapter 6, known as Dhyana Yoga, Gita establishes the foundations of mindfulness in a more integrative and comprehensive manner. Shlokas 1, 2, 3, and 4 of the Gita mention work with devotion as karma yoga. Karma Yoga purifies the human mind and enhances the chance of spiritual realization, peace and tranquility. A trained mind is the best friend of a person and an untrained mind is the worst enemy. The need to conquer the mind is supreme in Gita. Patanjali expresses it in terms of controlling the Chitta. The transactions of Chitta, or Manas or mind are to be controlled by balance in food, sleep, recreation and practice of prescribed duties. Meditation is for achieving steadiness of mind (Shlokas 20-23). Non-realization of *samadhi*, meditation leads to failure in achieving true knowledge and cycle of birth and rebirth. Equality in all beings with joy in their joy, and sorrow in their sorrows as if their own is the state of not self-awareness but awareness of others feelings, thoughts and suffering. Thus Gita also teaches a lesson in universal humanity by emphasizing the need of understanding emotions, feelings, sufferings of others and resolving them dutifully according to Dharma.

Although mindfulness is not used in the Gita in the same way researchers have used it achieving tangible mental and measurable outcomes. It is used as a way to live life and it is considered to be a central tendency of a Yogi or Siddha.

Awareness of the Present: awareness and knowledge are central to the Gita. Awareness of self is emphasized in many places. This self-awareness includes complete awareness of the senses and Manas (or Mind). By being aware of the senses and mind, a person keeps control over them and their transactions. Now the question is why controlling body, mind and senses is central for achieving peace and tranquility? The answer lies in the importance of addressing the instability of the mind. Shri Krishna says in several places in Gita that controlling the mind is the most difficult thing. It is stopping the flow of a storm and only by yoga and *Chitta Vritti Nirodha*, by controlling and disciplining the mind one can get closer to *Samadhi.* Now if we integrate the concept of a self-disciplined person to the structural power and prescriptive role of Dharma (the prescribed *Karma*) which is largely based on psycho-social reasoning for sustaining a productive peaceful society, we see that mental peace of a person depends on social factors. The conflict between sociocultural factors and individual interests creates a situation of stress and anxiety. Thus by disciplining the mind, teaching it self-containment and aligning the mind with social duties, Gita also provides a sociological device for maintaining peace in society.

Focused attention: A controlled mind can focus on the real cause and effect relationships in society and understand their consequences. An unfocussed mind can barely focus, observe, and understand the happenings around him. Mindfulness in the Gita, in this way is based on the principle of *Dhyana* means focusing your mind and the attention of the senses in understanding the true nature of society and the world. By focusing on real issues and subjects of knowledge one can achieve true understanding and nature of reality. The important thing Gita establishes in this context the role of understanding in achieving peace. Without understanding and proper knowledge, a person can't achieve lasting peace of mind. Perhaps the emphasis on gaining true knowledge in Gita is directly connected to the concept of Mindfulness as a central tenet. For attainment of knowledge, focus on real issues, observation and analysis are necessary conditions.

Non-judgmental awareness: Being non-judgmental is emphasized in Gita. Mindfulness theories recognize this dimension as an essential one in modern times. Why a non-judgmental mind can achieve focus and peace? Gita offers a way by proposing detachment as a mechanism. Detachment helps in being non-judgmental. By virtue of detachment a person, a seeker of knowledge or a researcher, can observe and understand without bias. Unbiased observation and reflection create true understanding. This concept resonates with the latest theories of knowledge in qualitative research such as, Phenomenology of Husserl (1931) where he advocates the bracketing of the researcher's judgments.

Self-reflection: Self-reflection can also be considered a kind of self-awareness. In Gita awareness of self is central and is mentioned in several places. For instance, Chapter 6 (Shloka, 15) emphasizes the need for a pure mind to see the true nature of Self or Atman. Observing self is possible only when one has withdrawn attention from the external world. Withdrawing senses from subjects is the first condition. This complete withdrawal implies that one, in the process of self-reflection and realization, should be able to focus on the internal cognitive processes only. The role of senses as input devices is restricted in this process and they must not be interfering in the process of reflection. This withdrawal is possible only by disciplining mind, developing a character endowed with self-containment, as a *Sadhak.*

Table 8 :Mindfulness in the Bhagavad Gita

Aspect	Explanation	Relevant Shlokas
Dhyana Yoga (Meditation)	Lord Krishna emphasizes focusing the mind on a single object or idea, restraining the restless mind to achieve tranquility and supreme happiness.	*Gita 6.35*: "The mind is restless and difficult to restrain, but it is subdued by practice and detachment."
		Gita 6.20: "When the mind becomes still and focused on the self, the yogi attains happiness and liberation."

Aspect	Explanation	Relevant Shlokas
		Gita 6.29: "The yogi sees the same supreme self in all beings and all beings in the self."
Devotion to God (Bhakti Yoga)	Chapter 12 highlights surrender and devotion to the divine will, emphasizing mindfulness as a key quality.	*Gita 12.1*: "The devotees who fix their minds on Me and worship Me with steadfast faith and devotion are the most perfect in yoga."
Dimensions of Mindfulness		
Awareness of the Present Moment	Being fully present without distractions from past or future thoughts.	*Gita 6.10*: "Hold body, neck, and head erect, gaze at the tip of the nose, remain steadfast in yoga, ever mindful of Me."
Focused Attention	Maintaining attention on a particular object or task without distractions.	*Gita 12.1*: "He who is devoted to me, who is of a controlled mind, who sees the same self in all beings, attains happiness."

Aspect	Explanation	Relevant Shlokas
Non-judgmental Awareness	Cultivating awareness of thoughts and emotions without getting caught up in them.	*Gita 6.14*: "With senses subdued, sees the self in all beings and divine everywhere."
Self-reflection	Engaging in introspection to understand oneself and the world.	*Gita 6.15*: "With a purified mind, sees oneself as the Self and realizes everything else is perishable."

Thus above section presents that dimensions of mindfulness in the Gita includes the importance of being fully present, focused attention, non-judgmental awareness and self-reflection. An individual can achieve a state of inner peace and spiritual enlightenment by practicing the mindfulness as stated in Gita.

CHAPTER 7

Self-Awareness as a Psychological Concept in Gita

Self in Indian Psychology

Upanishads draw a line between empirical self (Ego) and the true self of humans. This distinction has a significant implication for further philosophical discourses in Indian philosophy. Dissolving ego is necessary for nullifying the impact of empirical self on understanding the true self (Jacob, 1975). The empirical self is *Ahamkara*, and true self is Atman (the unchangeable, eternal, and pure consciousness underlying all existences according to Upanishads). Atman, or the true self or spirit is universal consciousness which creates a holistic unity between the individual and the cosmos (*Taittiriya* and *Brhadaranyaka Upanishads*). *Mandukya Upanishad* states different forms of consciousness as self. The *Atman* within humans reflects is the universal consciousness or Brahman which creates a holistic unity of human beings. Waking (*Vishwa*), Dream (*Taijasa*), Deep Sleep (Prajna) and Pure consciousness (Atman). The structure of the human psyche is described as consisting of the body (Sarira), mind (Manas), intellect (Buddhi), and vital principle (Prana), all united by Atman (*Mandukya Upanishad*).

Table 9 : Self-awareness in Srimad Bhagavad Gita

Aspect of Self	Description	Source/ Reference
Empirical Self (Ahamkara)	The ego, associated with the physical and mental aspects of existence, subject to change and suffering.	Upanishads
True Self (Atman)	The unchanging, eternal, and pure consciousness, underlying all existence.	Upanishads
Microcosm-Macrocosm Link	Atman within humans reflects the Brahman (universal consciousness), creating a holistic unity between the individual and the cosmos.	Taittiriya and Brhadaranyaka Upanishads
States of Consciousness	Waking (Visva), Dream (Taijasa), Deep Sleep (Prajna), and Pure Consciousness (Atman).	Mandukya Upanishad
Structure of the Psyche	Includes body (Sarira), mind (Manas), intellect (Buddhi), and vital principle (Prana), all united by Atman.	Samkhya and Yoga systems

Aspect of Self	Description	Source/ Reference
Relation to Cosmos	Atman (microcosm) mirrors Brahman (macrocosm); described through metaphors like two birds on a tree or the salt in water.	Mundaka and Chandogya Upanishads
Human Potential and Goal	Self-realization (Moksha or Nirvana) by transcending Ahamkara and aligning with Atman.	Upanishads, Vedanta, Jainism, Buddhism
Ethics and Dharma	Emphasizes ethical action and duty (Dharma) as aligned with cosmic order, essential for self-realization.	Bhagavad Gita, Mimamsa, and Epics
Unity in Duality	Coexistence of individuality (Jiva) and universality (Brahman) seen as either dualistic (Ramanuja, Madhava) or monistic (Sankara).	Vedanta philosophy
Holistic View	Integrates the body, mind, and spirit into an inseparable whole, rejecting Cartesian dualism.	Indian Philosophy as a whole

Aspect of Self	Description	Source/ Reference
Self as Experiential Reality	Knowledge of Atman attained through direct experience (Anubhava) rather than intellectual understanding alone.	Sankara's Advaita Vedanta

Self-Awareness as a Psychological Concept in Gita

Self-awareness refers to the ability to have a clear and accurate perception of oneself. Self-awareness is considered the foundation of self-knowledge. Understanding the inner self is pivotal to understanding the external world. Self-knowledge begins with self-observation. Self-observation is followed by self-examination and self-evaluation. It is said that understanding of the world depends on understanding the self.

The western discourse of understanding the self is characterized by several theoretical frameworks. The Psychoanalytic Theory of the Self understands that the self emerges through unconscious drives and conflicts and divides the self into the id, ego, and superego. The ego is the mediating factor between desires and social norms (Freud, 1923). Social Identity Theory emphasizes that self-concept is developed by group membership, intergroup interactions, and dynamics. Individuals derive identity from social groups, which plays an important role in shaping identity. It affects our behavior and self-perception, with social norms, interactions, and constructions having an important influence on the self of a person (Tajfel & Turner, 1979). The Symbolic Interactionist Perspective emphasizes that the self develops through social interaction and symbolic communication by using language and symbols. Thus, the self emerges through social interaction and symbolic communication. The subjective self ("I") and social self ("Me") are developed through societal engagement and interaction (Mead, 1934). Self-Determination Theory (SDT) highlights the importance of intrinsic needs for autonomy, competence, and relatedness and focuses on how the fulfillment of these needs fosters authentic self-development and psychological well-being (Deci & Ryan, 1985). Narrative Identity Theory proposes that the self is constructed through personal narratives and life stories. The self is a narrative identity in which individuals create meaning through their personal stories (McAdams, 1997). *Looking-Glass Self Theory* provides a perspective that self-concept is formed through others' perceptions and reactions. It posits that individuals see themselves through the mirror of others' judgments (Cooley, 1902). Cultural Psychology of the Self proposes that self-concept varies across different cultures. The theory suggests that the Western individualistic self is distinct from the Eastern collectivistic self (Kitayama & Markus, 1991). Ego Identity Theory emphasizes the development of the self through psychosocial development across life stages (Erikson, 1959). The Ecological Self arises through interactions with the environment and is grounded in sensory and physical experiences with the world (Neisser, 1988). The True and False Self Theory differentiates between the authentic self and the defensive self. The true self reflects authentic feelings, whereas the false self arises from social compliance and defense mechanisms (Winnicott, 1960).

Ancient Greek Views on the Self

The nature of self is explored in western perspectives of Greek and Roman cultures. These views focus on following nature for a harmonious and meaningful life. Stoic-Epicurean views of self present it as the development of reason, virtue, and emotion linking it to an ethical character. These views are basically defined by their focus on understanding character to comprehend the self of a person. Character could be identified by behavioral patterns in different crisis situations or real-life problems. It could be contrasted with the Platonic-Aristotelian view separating psyche and body. Plato's concept of the soul as immortal and an image of god emphasizes virtue and rationality with embodied states of the soul. In fact it was Plato who popularized the concept of the tripartite self, which is composed of bodily self, spiritual self and intellectual self represented by bodily appetite (Bodily self), emotions (Spirit or Heart) and Intellect (Intellectual self). Aristotle emphasizes virtuous reasoning and self-care as integral to relationships with other. The focus on harmonious living by interconnectedness aligns well with today's psychosocial theories. Plato and Aristotle discuss the dichotomy of rational and irrational forces in contrast with epicurean holistic views. Biological energy in psyche-body interconnectedness is evident in Stoic views which emphasize understanding the soul as inseparable from the body. This is in line with the ancient medical techniques which saw body and soul inseparable. The body and soul are integrated. Inner harmony is emphasized for virtue, aligning of emotions and reason for ethical living. To be virtuous is to act in accordance with an inner feeling of harmony. It connects that virtuousness is related to ethical beliefs and reasoning. In Greek culture both Plato and the Stoic views present universe as rational and providential construction. They visualize the world as a cosmic unity of psyche and body (Christensen, 2024). The ethical failures in realizing self are derived from disruptions in natural development which is tied to passions and psychic illness. Perhaps Freud has taken inspiration from ancient Greek views about the psychic energy and its connections with passions and desires. Stoic and Epicurean philosophers visualized humans as integrated psyche-body wholes and proposed the psychophysical holism. Human beings and other human animals are related to complex constructed psychological-physical unities or wholes (Christensen, 2024).

Christian and Medieval Views on the Self

Christian theology played a significant role in shaping the concept of self in the medieval period. This age was dominated by clerics and theological discourses. Thus, the medieval self was deeply rooted in the theological framework of Christianity. In Christianity, the self is considered a divine creation of God. It encompasses intellect and free will. The theological basis positions it as inherently moral, serving divine purposes (White, 1978). The self was understood primarily in connection to the divine purpose as a part of the whole creation. The creator endowed humans with intellect and free will (White, 1978). Christianity understands selfhood within a divine context (Harbus, 2002).

The self was a moral agency tasked with ethical action and judgment under the divine law of Biblical commandments. Confession reinforced moral self-examination, and the self embodied restraint and ethical control (White, 1978). These medieval views align with the Gita, which considers self as a divine construct and emphasizes disciplining of the self. Connection to the soul was a central point of self in the medieval age. Medieval selfhood was intertwined with the soul but included a secular character and thought focused on self-exploration beyond spiritual boundaries (Harbus, 2002)

The self is also seen as a process, a dynamic reshaping through memory, moral struggles, divine purpose, and piety. Memory shapes the evolving self, and Christian rituals emphasized personal reform and spiritual growth (White, 1978). A cosmic connection can be established between the self and the broader environment. The self can be considered as a part of the macrocosm, which reflects the divine order and is influenced by planetary and cosmic forces. Astrology and cosmology linked personal destiny with the celestial order (White, 1978), and the self could be considered a microcosm mirroring divine creation (Harbus, 2002).

The urbanization of Europe saw changes in infrastructure and architecture, which focused on individuality. This provided room for thinking in solitude. Innovations like chimneys created physical spaces for private reflection and supported individualism and identity (White, 1978). The role of science could be understood in terms of the assumption that the self was engaged with understanding the divine laws through scientific inquiry. The self felt tension between empirical science and subjective spiritual experiences. Further, the development of scientific paradigms for understanding the self was emphasized in the modern period after the Renaissance (White, 1978). Augustine saw the self as fundamentally flawed and in need of divine grace for salvation. Being influenced by Platonic concept of self, he proposed a hierarchical view of the self with reason on the top controlling other aspects.

These Christian and medieval views on the self shaped the discourse of selfhood in modern western perspectives. Self was seen as a fallen and sinful soul which needs redemption by using reason and faith as complementary to each other. This continued to shape philosophical and theological debates in the Western world.

Renaissance Humanism and the Emergence of Modern Self

The Renaissance period in Europe marked a shift in the concept of self. The emergence of the individual as an autonomous entity is distinct from the collective identities portrayed in the medieval period. Foucault (1973) saw the Renaissance as the period of the emergence of modern man, highlighting the centrality of man and his capacity for self-introspection. Chessick (2010) proposes the development of a private self that was independent of societal validation. Art was seen as a mirror of the self during the Renaissance period. The transition from flat and symbolic representations of Gothic art to realistic and emotionally rich depictions of individual selfhood could be seen (Masaccio's The Expulsion from the Garden of Eden, as cited in Chessick, 2010). The influence of the individual self is also evident in literature, where the exploration of complex, layered selves in Shakespeare's characters embodies internal conflicts and authenticity (Bloom, 1998). Philosophical underpinnings of the Renaissance self emerged from the rediscovery of classical texts. Humanists such as Pico della Mirandola argued for man's unique position as a creation of free will, capable of shaping his own destiny (Chessick, 2010). This perspective led to the development of an autochthonous self, rooted in existential authenticity and internal coherence. The psychoanalytical perspective on self offers deep insights into the Renaissance self. Works by Freud, Winnicott, and Modell lead in this exploration. Freud's concept of the "I" and the unconscious parallels the Renaissance focus on introspection and the hidden depths of human personality (Freud, 1933). Winnicott's (1965) idea of the true self resonates with the Renaissance emphasis on individuality as an authentic and inviolable core. Chessick (2010) elaborates that the transition from medieval to Renaissance notions of self can be explored as a movement from an externally defined self to an internally driven self and autonomy.

Renaissance humanism emphasized the dignity and autonomy of the individual self and highlighted reason, free will and human agency. Human possess freedom and creative potential to shape their destiny, making a shift from the sinful self of medieval age. It provided a foundation for modern self by focusing on human potential and individuality during the Renaissance. It introduced the dualism by separating mind and body. The self was defined as tabula rasa (blank slate) which is shaped by sensory experience and environmental factors. It rejects the notion of innate identity which could not be altered and rejects the deterministic notion of self. Kant incorporated the concept of transcendental self in his critique of pure reason. He proposed that self is a transcendental condition for the possibility of experience and it shapes actively our perceptions and is a subject of inquiry, not an object.

These enlightenment philosophers have laid the foundation for the modern concept of self as a rational, creative, autonomous and active agent which is capable of shaping its own identity and understanding of the world.

Existentialism and the Search for Authentic Self

In the 19th and 20th centuries, the concept of self was expanded by existentialism. Influential thinkers like Kierkegaard, Nietzsche, Sartre, and Simone de Beauvoir focused on the individual's search for meaning, authenticity, and freedom (Rice, 1950; Tubbs, 2013). They identified the role of absurdity in human existence. Exploration of self should begin with subjective experiences (Rice, 1950; Tubbs, 2013). Subjectivity, as a starting point of philosophy and self was considered a cornerstone for discovering its place in non-human and social contexts (Rice, 1950). The self was considered existence and prioritized over essence. The self defines itself through existence and actions, rather than being defined by any pre-existing essence and deterministic notion of human life and meaning. Sartre's dictum "existence precedes essence" defines the core of existential philosophy (Rice, 1950). Human freedom is an essential and central aspect of existentialism. The freedom of the self comes with the burden of being free. It implies that individuals are responsible for their own actions (Sartre, cited in Tubbs, 2013). The self encounters its own freedom through interactions with others, often leading to conflict (Rice, 1950). The role of conflict in the evolution of self is central in existential philosophy. Although a sense of social solidarity arises in crisis, existential individuality prevents permanent unity (Rice, 1950). The self is experienced through the body in action and hence is an embodied concept. It cannot be seen as a passive physical entity. The body is a nucleus of living significations that are central to its engagement with the world (Merleau-Ponty, cited in Rice, 1950). Sartre's notion of nausea reflects the self's confrontation with the absurdity of existence and the nothingness at its core (Sartre, cited in Rice, 1950). Consciousness of the self is driven by an incompleteness or void that propels the self towards becoming (Rice, 1950). The self struggles between essence and existence and reflects the educational perspective of "know thyself" (Tubbs, 2013). Education mediates the self's tension between individuality and universality (Tubbs, 2013). The self is historically constructed and defined through interpersonal relationships and cultural norms (Rice, 1950; Tubbs, 2013). Political and social engagements are inevitable parts of self-discovery, and sociopolitical action is of a tragic and uncertain nature (Rice, 1950; Tubbs, 2013) .

Existentialist philosophy challenged traditional notions of the self. It denied the concept of the self as a fixed, objective entity and emphasized the subjective and individual aspects of human existence. It highlighted the significance of individual freedom, choice, and responsibility in shaping the self.

Concept of Self in Postmodernism

In the late 20th century, postmodernism challenged the notion of a unified, coherent self. Michel Foucault, Jacques Derrida, and Judith Butler played an important role in this discourse.

The self is depicted as fragmented across various contexts and influences. Jameson's (1991) concept of the fragmented postmodern subject. Lovett's conflicting schemas of feeling responsible for others vs. inability to fight the system. Multiplicity of individuals internalized diverse and contradictory schemas. For example Monteiro's cultural pride and independence could be juxtaposed with her rejection of patriarchal ideas. Although the self is fragmented, individuals often exhibit partial coherence through emotional or habitual schemas. Early life experiences and events shape enduring schemas that influence adult identities and interpretations. For example, Russo's childhood shaped her victimization schema (Ortner, 1991). Contextual shaping of identity is justified. The self is shaped in response to specific interview contexts or social expectations. Role of public discourses and cultural narratives is important in the conceptualization of the self. Emotional concerns such as safety, love and status, provide consistency amidst diverse experiences. Identities are constructed and adapted through interactions, storytelling and cultural contexts. Thus postmodernism challenges to the idea of a stable cantered self, replacing it with dynamic and situational identities.

Table 10: Concept of Self in Modern Psychology

Aspect	Description
Fragmentation of Self	The self is no longer seen as unified but fragmented across various contexts and influences.
Multiplicity of Schemas	Individuals internalize diverse, often contradictory cultural schemas.
Integration Amidst Fragmentation	Despite fragmentation, individuals often exhibit partial coherence through emotional or habitual schemas.
Influence of Early Experiences	Early life events shape enduring schemas that influence adult identities and interpretations.
Contextual Shaping of Identity	The self is shaped in response to specific interview contexts or social expectations.
Role of Public Discourses	Public discourses and cultural narratives influence the individual's conceptualization of self.
Emotional and Social Drivers	Emotional concerns (e.g., safety, love, status) provide consistency amidst diverse experiences.
Self as a Negotiated Construct	Identities are constructed and adapted through interactions, storytelling, and cultural contexts.

Aspect	Description
Critique of Unified Self	Challenges to the idea of a stable, centered self, replaced by dynamic, situational identities.
Role of Memory and Narratives	Memory is selective and influenced by current schemas, linking past and present in edited narratives.

The concept of Self is continuously evolving in Western discourses. It raises new questions and challenges traditional notions of identity, authenticity and agency. With questioning the very foundations of human existence and experience which starts from understanding one's self; post modernism prompts us to critically examine our understanding of self and its relationship with the world. It also invites further exploration and inquiry into the nature of human existence.

CHAPTER 8

Concept of Self in Gita

Following verses are relevant to understanding the concept of self in the Gita

Shloka 29 of Chapter 6 renunciates the undivided and presence of same self in all beings. One needs to understand that the universal self reflects in all human beings and this provides a principle of oneness of human beings. "The Self is the Same in All Beings.. (Gita 6.29)"

Self-discovery in the Gita gives emphasis on disciplining the mind through yoga and fixing it on inner reflection without any intervention from outer world. Yoga is instrumental in fixing and controlling the mind on the real subject of knowledge. Self is the real subject of knowledge. It can be understood by reflection and focused contemplation (Gita 6.15)

Chapter 2 sheds light on immortal nature of the human self. It is never born and never dies. It is unborn, eternal, ever-existing, perennial, and primeval. Self can be seen as a microcosm (smallest) and a macrocosm (the greatest). It is situated in every living and human being (Gita Chapter 8, Shloka 4). Self is the main driving force in life. If one can control and discipline it, then it would be his dearest friend and guide. Otherwise, an uncontrolled, undisciplined, and outward-focused self would be the cause of destruction of the person

(Gita 6.6). Controlling one's mind and self helps one remain calm in the situation of crisis. Controlling senses gives peace and stability in the situation of sorrow, pain or crisis. A person remains calm and controlled during honor and dishonor. Gita teaches the self as a stable, immutable, and immortal identity beyond this physical world and connects it to the Supreme Self or Krishna (Chapter 6, Shloka 7). Supreme Self dwells in the heart of all beings (Chapter 18, Shloka 61). Becoming self-content is one necessity in Yoga and for it, a person needs to give up all desires arising in the mind and become content (Chapter 2, Shloka 55). The focus on being self-content and self-containment is common in Gita. It is due to yogic persona of Krishna. As the greatest yogi, Shri Krishna often talks about controlling desires, limiting them, understanding the true nature which is same in all beings and supreme god Krishna.

Chapter 4, Shloka 18 explains how there is action within inaction and inaction within action and only self is unchanging between this action and inaction. If Arjuna or any individual does action without attachment and according to prescribed Dharma, his actions don't accumulate Karma. These actions or Karma liberate him, frees him from anxiety and conflicts. There is another possible explanation of the Shloka which focuses on withdrawal from the duties. As Arjuna fears to fight, hesitate to raise voice for the justice or Dharma's prescribed duties of a Kshatriya for a call to war. Krishna explains him that if you withdraw, you think that you are avoiding Karma; but it is not exactly like that. The opposite side is that if you don't fight you accumulate Adharma or Sins. Why so? Because if you don't oppose evil, you encourage him. You are committing the same sin by encouraging evil while being silent or neutral. This is the main logic on which the exposition resides. Withdrawal of duties may seem an inaction, but it is a bad and evil action.

While performance of duty as prescribed, is considered pious and way to liberation. Fight for glory, die for duty.

In conclusion, the concept of Self in Gita provides a profound and transformative understanding of the nature of existence and purpose of life. It provides the way to access the ternal and divine side of human existence and a practical solution to peace and tranquility.

Table 11: Concept of Self in Gita vs. Modern Perspectives (According to Bhavuk, 2005)

Aspect of Self	Components/Concepts	Description	Citations/References
Metaphysical Self	**Atman**	Eternal, indestructible, immutable, beyond time and space; the true self and the ultimate goal is to realize and unite with Brahman.	Bhagavad Gita (2:17–22, 2:24–25), Shankaracharya's Sivoham Stotra, Taittiriya Upanishad, Paranjpe (1984, 1998)
Social Self	**Caste, Social Roles, Relationships**	Defined through social constructs like caste and life stages (ashramas); reflects interdependence.	Bhawuk (2004, 2005), Sinha (1965), Bhagavad Gita (7:4, 15:7), Indian Ashrama System
Physical Self	**Body (Annamaya Kosha)**	Material aspect of self; vehicle for spiritual practice; recognized in Ayurveda, yoga, and daily rituals.	Taittiriya Upanishad (Pancha Kosha model), Yoga traditions, Vedic Sandhya, Ayurveda (Kapha, Vata, Pitta), Durga Saptashati, Bhagavad Gita (3:40, 6:14)

Aspect of Self	Components/Concepts	Description	Citations/References
Mind (Manas)	**Cognition, Emotion, Behavioral Intent**	The seat of cognition, emotions, and action; intermediary between senses and intellect; focus of discipline and meditation.	Yajurveda (34.1–34.6), Bhagavad Gita (1:30, 2:55–67, 6:12–35, 8:10–12), Prabhupada (1986), Sinha & Tripathi (1994)
Intellect (Buddhi)	**Discrimination, Decision-making, Direction**	Guides self-realization by discriminating between eternal and transient; helps in focusing manas inwardly.	Bhagavad Gita (2:39–49, 3:40–43, 6:25, 18:29–32), Paranjpe (1984, 1998), Adi Shankaracharya's commentary
Ego (Ahamkara)	**Sense of Agency**	Individual agency essential for worldly life; an obstacle in spiritual realization.	Bhagavad Gita (7:4, 13:5), Vivekachudamani, Yogavasistha

Aspect of Self	Components/Concepts	Description	Citations/References
Sheaths of Self	**Pancha Koshas**	Layers of self: Annamaya (physical), Pranamaya (vital), Manomaya (mental), Vijnanamaya (intellectual), Anandamaya (blissful).	Taittiriya Upanishad, Pancha Kosha model
Spiritual Journey	**Union with Brahman (Moksha)**	Focus on transcending the physical and social selves to realize Atman.	Bhagavad Gita (2:17–25, 8:10–12), Sivoham Stotra, Bhawuk (2008)
Cultural Constructs	**Regional Identities, Norm-driven Concepts (Dharma, Yajna, Tapas)**	Embedded in regional identities, social values, and norms (e.g., dharma, yajna).	Mohanty (2007), Durga Saptashati, Bhagavad Gita (17:11–16)
Environmental Context	**External (Five Elements), Internal (Manas, Buddhi, Ahamkara)**	External elements (earth, fire, water, air, space) interact with internal components of self.	Bhagavad Gita (7:4–7, 15:7, 15:9), Sankhya Philosophy

Chapter 9
Self-Regulation

Self-regulation is an individual's ability to control thoughts, feelings, and behaviors. It helps in achieving long-term goals and objectives. It involves the regulation of emotions, impulses, and attention of persons during normal life and in crisis as well. It can be defined as the ability to delay gratification and resist temptation.

One of the most widely used models of self-regulation is the Strengths and Weaknesses of Self-Regulation (SWSR) model. Self-Regulation can be defined as the ability to consciously control, monitor and modify one's thoughts, emotions, behavior. In educational psychology, it is viewed through the lens of self-regulated learning (SRL) as a process involving goal-setting, planning, monitoring and evaluation (Pintrich, 2000). In the context of health psychology it is defined as a set of deliberate actions to modify one's behavior in line with health goals. It also focuses on effortful and goal-directed actions (Hagger, 2010). Thus, self regulation is a goal-driven, effortful process essential for understanding educational and health-related behavior. Role of goals is important in this process. Goals keep the focus as a central driving force for initiating and sustaining goal-oriented actions. In education, focus is on academic goals such as mastering a subject or improving study habits. Goals are often constructed by teachers and students.

In health psychology goals are health-oriented and tied to long-term health outcomes. Goals must be contextually relevant. Key processes and mechanisms involved in self-regulation are goal setting, monitoring, planning, feedback and reflection. It includes cognitive and metacognitive, behavioral, and motivational components including self-efficacy. Individual capacity and contextual support is necessary for self-regulation. Failures in self-regulation occur when individuals cannot bridge the gap between intentions and actions due to lack of resources, conflicting goals and cognitive overload. Challenges include cognitive overload, lack of emotional regulation and poorly defined goals (Martin & McLellan, 2007). Thus, self-regulation is a foundational construct involving cognitive, emotional and behavioral coordination to achieve desired outcomes and goals in life.

Self-Regulation in Gita

Gita focuses on self-realization. Thus, self-regulation is the key process in achieving self-realization. This includes the realization of the Self (Atman) as eternal consciousness and aligning actions with self-knowledge for self-mastery. The self-regulation is portrayed as self-mastery in Gita (Chapter 2, Shloka 55; Chapter 5, Shloka 24). Thus Gita combines psychological processes with spiritual purpose of self-realization. Goal setting is also an important step in self-regulation in Western theories. Gita calls one to follow Swadharma (One's prescribed duty) and Nishkama Karma which comprises selfless action and emphasizes meaningful ethical goals (*Chapter 3, Shloka 35; Chapter 6, Shloka 5*). Integrating goal-setting and spiritual ethical alignment and personal responsibility for societal welfare in Gita is a unique blend of understanding the behavior of the individual and functioning of society. Emotional regulation is depicted as

SthitPragya (Resolute Intelligence or Steady Wisdom) which is achieved by detachment from outcomes. Gita by detaching the individual from outcomes, provides the way to deal with absurdity in human life.

Table 12: Self-Regulation in Srimad Bhagavad Gita

Aspect	Findings from Second Paper (Bhagavad Gita)	Implications
Definition of Self-Regulation	The realization of the Self (*Atman*) as eternal consciousness and aligning actions with self-knowledge for self-mastery (*Chapter 2, Shloka 55; Chapter 5, Shloka 24*).	Combines psychological focus on behavioral control with the Gita's spiritual emphasis on self-realization and purpose.
Goal Setting	*Swadharma* (one's duty) and *Nishkama Karma* (selfless action) emphasize meaningful, ethical goals (*Chapter 3, Shloka 35; Chapter 6, Shloka 5*).	Integrates goal-setting with ethical alignment and personal responsibility for societal welfare.
Emotional Regulation	*Sthitaprajna* (steady wisdom) emphasizes emotional stability through detachment from outcomes and dualities (*Chapter 2, Shlokas 48, 55-57*).	Combines emotional regulation strategies with spiritual equanimity to manage emotions effectively.

Aspect	Findings from Second Paper (Bhagavad Gita)	Implications
Behavioral Regulation	*Karma Yoga* stresses disciplined action and the purification of the mind through selfless deeds (*Chapter 3, Shlokas 8, 19; Chapter 18, Shloka* 45).	Aligns disciplined behavior with selfless service for holistic self-regulation.
Mechanisms of Regulation	Practices like *Shravana* (listening), *Manana* (reflection), and *Nididhyasana* (meditation) enhance self-regulation (*Chapter 6, Shlokas 6, 1*5).	Integrates structured mechanisms with contemplative practices for deeper, sustained self-regulation.
Challenges	Ignorance, attachment, and dominance of *Rajas* and *Tamas* hinder self-regulation (*Chapter 14, Shlokas 5-8; Chapter 3, Shlokas 36-37*).	Adds a spiritual dimension to addressing challenges, focusing on overcoming attachment and ignorance through *Sattva*.
Social Implications	*Lokasangraha* (welfare of society) emphasizes self-regulation as a path to collective good and moral leadership (*Chapter 3, Shlokas 20-21*).	Broadens the societal role of self-regulation by incorporating ethical and spiritual responsibilities.

Aspect	Findings from Second Paper (Bhagavad Gita)	Implications
Applications to Education	Aligning educational goals with self-awareness and character building through *Swadharma* (*Chapter 18, Shloka 45; Chapter 6, Shloka* 5).	Enhances educational practices by incorporating self-awareness and ethical dimensions into learning.

Behavioral regulation as part of self-regulation in Gita is achieved through Karma Yoga which stresses disciplined action and purification of the mind through selfless deeds and samadhi (*Chapter 3, Shlokas 8, 19; Chapter 18, Shloka 45*). It aligns disciplined behavior with selfless service for holistic self-regulation and expansion of the self. The mechanisms of regulation in Gita include practices like *Shravana* (listening), *Manana* (reflection), and *Nididhyasana* (meditation) enhance self-regulation (*Chapter 6, Shlokas 6, 15*). These practices integrate structured mechanisms with contemplative practices for deeper sustained self-regulation. Gita also provides description of challenges in practicing self-regulation and control. Ignorance of a person, attachment and dominance of Rajas and Tamas traits in human personality are responsible for hindering self-regulation (Chapter 14, Shlokas 5-8; Chapter 3, Shlokas 36-37). It adds a spiritual dimension to addressing challenges, focusing on overcoming attachment and ignorance through practice of yoga and promoting Sattvik traits and behavior. Social implications of self-regulation is the broader well-being of society which is depicted as Lokasangraha. Lord Krishna himself says " I don't have any duty to perform in this world, but I reincarnate myself and work like an ordinary man to present and example of dutifulness and Karma.

These principles of self-regulation in Gita have broader educational implications which align educational goals with self-awareness and character building through Swadharma (*Chapter 18, Shloka 45; Chapter 6, Shloka 5*). *Swadharme Nidhanam Shreyas* (It is better to die for your duties in society) which Ghalib appreciates

"Wafadari Basharte Ustuwari Asl E Imaan hai, Mare butkhane me to Kabe me Gado Birahaman Ko". If a Brahmin dies performing his duties honestly in a temple, he should be buried in the Kaba (The Islamic symbol of spirituality). The mutual appreciation of cultural values in India has been a long tradition and characteristic of its inclusive culture.

Chapter 10
A Model of Psychological Process in Gita

The Bhagwat Gita offers a general model and outline of psychological processes. It begins with the reflection of the true nature of human self and then about Dharma and prescribed duties of human beings in society

Exploration of psychological processes in Gita can take two perspectives. One, going inductively without any theoretical lens and the second is understanding the practices and statements of Gita with reference to present psychological frameworks and theories. The best approach should combine both approaches for providing an integrated view on psychology in Gita. One can understand the psychology of the human being from different perspectives of Behaviorism, Cognitivism, and social constructivism. These theoretical frameworks provide useful insights about processes of mind and self. The central focus in Gita is on understanding the causes of human desire. No one can deny the role of desires and their relationship with human suffering in practical life and social world. Human desire can obscure the pursuit of real knowledge. It is interesting that the mainstream literature on happiness doesn't consider desire's role like Gita's centrality on it. Now setting aside desires by controlling them, Gita offers a way of Karmayoga—the selfless duty detached from the expectation of outcomes. Karmayoga can be said an antidote to the uncontrolled desires and resulted frustration and anger. Gita establishes the most important role of Karma in human life. Karma can be compared to the concept of agency in western sociology and psychology. Contemplating the desired or unexpected results while performing duties can psychologically obstruct and interfere with the understanding of the task and its performance. Logically it would impact the action and its effectiveness. According to Bhagavad Gita one achieves mental peace when he or she ceases to be concerned about the outcomes of one's efforts. This is about giving 100% of your capacity, with pure mind without any fear of result or anxiety of performance. What one can do is to devote his hundred percent towards his work. This state of *Sthitpragyata* or bliss within occurs when a person attains liberation from cognition, emotion and behavior and even happiness. Happiness is only an emotion which is short-lasting. Gita provides an everlasting mechanism for work, life and happiness. The purity and stability of Chitta or Manas is the source of all happiness and tranquility. The momentous happiness is not eternal or everlasting. It is fragile, sensational and often distracting from the broader goals of individual and society. It is only through the renunciation of all desires that the individual can enter this state and stay content within his/her true self or the atman.

In the Bhagavad Gita, desires orginate from interactions between sense organs, Manas, and Buddhi which then engage with the body and allow the self to perceive and comprehend the environment and decide the course of action. The self choses some elements form the environment to which it eventually attaches itself, and the inclusion of cognitive and affective elements in this attachment results in the formation of a desire. The model of psychological processes within Gita draws upon the ancient Indian tradition of *Patanjal Yog*. In the Gita, it is said that the earth does not have sufficient resources for fulfilling the desires of a greedy Human. Thus, satisfying on minimal necessities as per Dharma is the only option for sustainability of society and environment. It emphasizes the insatiable needs of an unawaken person and provides solution as limiting one's desires and self-control.

If we contemplate the source of desires and their outcomes we can easily understand that fulfilment of desires has a positive effect that results in emotions of achievement. The unfulfillment of these desires results in negative effect and frustration. It is asserted in the Bhagavad Gita that even positive emotions arising from achieving desires lead to unhappiness in the long run because desires are inherently unsatisfying. Fulfillment of one desire leads to the birth of new and higher-order desires. These new and multiple desires create new tensions and sources of negative affect. All pleasures that are derived from the contact between body and environment essentially entail distress in short or long run. This distress is pervasive. Similarly, Buddha found that the essence of the life is *Dukkha (Suffering)* and one has to overcome it with the prescribed ways of Buddhism. Although Gita never says that the essence of life is Dukkha but positively talks about understanding the root causes of it. The root cause is desire which comes from uncontrolled, unmediated interactions lacking intelligence causing immense and illogical desires which are not socially approved or sanctioned by Dharma.

The pursuit of desires should be checked by *Viveka (The resolute intelligence)* otherwise it causes unhappiness. The mainstream literature on happiness and subjective well-being does not include this concept. Instead, Karmayoga, or the Path of the Work, is a better way to see and take decisions in life.

Self-reflection and contemplation have been major strategies to understand the right and wrong decisions in life. To follow the path of Karmayoga, to avoid the shackles of desires, we must undergo self-reflection and contemplation. Gita ranks Dhyana or meditation higher than the path of knowledge. Knowledge alone cannot bring the desired change if a person has not mastered his senses, mind and its distracting functions. Giving up the fruits of one's effort and giving the credit to god or society at large as described by Dharma, is part of Dhyana. Giving up the luring subjects of senses, giving up the desired outcomes and engaging oneself in understanding the true nature of his own personality is the need in the Gita. The problems of social sciences and psychology are basically focused on positive principles on observable outcomes and behaviors; but Gita focuses on understanding the root causes of the problem—the desires and their origins. According to the Bhagavad Gita, the state of tranquility or equanimity is known as sthitaprajna which comes after Dhyana and righteous conduct.

In addition, the Bhagavad Gita highlights the role of self-reflection and contemplation as a means of increasing awareness of one's desires; and their regulation. The key to happiness is not material possession, nor unending fulfillment of physical desires. The only key is controlling the senses, understanding the true self, purification of self and non-attached observation of the world. It is quite in line with the modern qualitative approach of research which emphasizes observation of context or world with being aware of your own limitations and prejudices of self. Self is the first thing to locate in the process of knowing and understanding the reality. Self should be the starting point of any knowledge pursuit. Without clarifying the assumptions, foundations and mechanisms of self and its role in the process of knowing is incomplete.

Overall, the Bhagavad Gita's model of psychological processes and desire proposes a unique perspective about understanding the nature of reality, self and human behavior. It does not only have explanatory power, but it also has the potential to guide the practical life. By following the path of Karmayoga, one can truly achieve the control on desires, anxiety caused by the outcome of action and maintain everlasting happiness and liberation.

Chapter 11
Resilience

Resilience refers to an individual's capacity to recover from adversities and adapt to new strategies of stress management. It is crucial for mental well-being and self-development. It focuses on survival, recovery, and thriving. It has been found crucial for mental well-being, physical health, academic success, and job performance.

Definition of Resilience

Resilience in Mahabharata could be seen from historical and modern perspectives in the Gita. The Gita conceptualizes resilience as a dynamic interplay of persistence and acceptance in the face of adversity. Resilience is examined in the situation of adversity. Garg (2019) used Foucauldian Discourse Analysis (FDA) to examine resilience in the Gita's verses. She identified key discourses about resilience in the Gita as the pursuit of emotional and spiritual progress (Attainment), overcoming attachment, anger, fear, and grief (Letting Go), mastery over desires and senses to achieve stability of mind (Control), and continuous self-improvement through knowledge and wisdom (Learning). The practical implications include encouraging detachment from results (Karma Yoga) and equanimity in outcomes (victory or defeat). It promotes self-discipline and surrender to a higher purpose. Its significance lies in providing insights for personal growth and psychological well-being.

Factors which Contribute to Resilience

Individual Factors: Individual factors are responsible for resilience. These are optimism, self-esteem, emotional regulation, and self-efficacy (Lamond et al., 2018). In Shloka 5 of Chapter 6, it is said that a person can uplift himself by his own. Self is the greatest enemy and also greatest friend also. This indicates the importance of individual factors in resilience for encouraging personal growth and self-improvement to enhance resilience.

Social and Environmental Factors: Social and environmental factors play an important role in resilience. Social support (Family, friends, community), access to resources, and exposure to moderate stress are significant predictors of resilience. If we see the journey of Arjuna and Krishna in Mahabharata, it is well proved that Arjuna's character acquired significant resources before the War. He went for meditation, tapas, and secured several weapons of war (Agneyastra, Narayanastra, and other protective measures). Resourcefulness is also a characteristic of resilience. The support from Arjuna's family, friends, and warrior community made him fight the war.

Common Themes of Resilience in Mahabharata and Gita: Kumari (2019) explored resilience through characters in Mahabharata, emphasizing their ability to navigate crises and setbacks. The central character is Krishna, who could be seen as a strategist and exemplar of resilience and inspiring others to act righteously. Krishna's life has several crises, from his birth in jail and then being nurtured by a non-biological mother. Being separated from his biological parents, Krishna faces numerous crises in his childhood, attacks from demons, conspiracies to be killed, and many more. Krishna deals with all these adversities with a calm mind and a smile.

Furthermore, Kumari (2019) writes about Karna, who was abandoned by his mother Kunti after birth. Karna shows several instances of resilience from his birth, abandonment, learning, and fighting for his own side. Karna rises above adversities and becomes a king. A fierce warrior, Karna's life is an exemplar of how to survive and come out of crises. His belief in his abilities and strong discipline and training makes him one of the most invincible warriors in Mahabharata. Arjuna could be seen as a case of resilience also. His transformation from despair to action under Krishna's guidance showcases psychological resilience.

Pandey and Mishra (2021) explored Gita's philosophical teachings as a foundation for resilience. According to them, resilience is framed through three Yogas in Gita:

Gyan Yoga (Knowledge): Emphasizes understanding the transient nature of life.

Karma Yoga (Action): Focuses on detachment from the fruits of actions, promoting emotional stability.

Bhakti Yoga (Devotion): Emphasizes divine connection as a resource for overcoming challenges.

The Role of Resilience in Various Domains

In chapter 18, Shloka 66, Krishna tells Arjuna to surrender himself to God. This surrender to God or Krishna meaning that if a person is fully devoted to his duties without any kind of attachment, they would emerge resilient.

Conclusion

Common themes of resilience in Mahabharata and Gita indicate that resilience is a multifaceted concept involving traits like adaptability, control, and equanimity. It is also a dynamic process influenced by external factors such as relationships and spirituality.

Concept of Resilience in Gita

Chapter 2, Shloka 14: Emphasizes enduring life's ups and downs.

Chapter 12, Shlokas 6-7: Describe devotion to Krishna for resilience and liberation. In Chapter 12, devotion is seen as a resilience tool, while Chapter 2 emphasizes understanding the transient nature of life.

Chapter 18, Shloka 66: Krishna advises surrendering to God, highlighting that devotion to duties without attachment fosters resilience.

Insights on Resilience from the Bhagavad Gita and Mahabharata Integrated with Theories of Resilience

Overall, these shlokas from Bhagavad Gita offer practical and valuable insights into the nature of resilience and its importance for mental health. They suggest that a resilient person develops a sense of equanimity and detachment towards expectations of Karma and engages in a detached stance with life. He takes both victory and defeat equally, and does his best. By reducing reliance on sensual pleasures and understanding the transient nature of things and feelings in this world, a resilient person remains stable and calm. By incorporating these insights into their practice, a person can cultivate the inner strength and stability needed to thrive in the face of adversity.

Table 13 : A Comparative Overview of Resilience in Srimad Bhagavad Gita

Aspect	Key Insights from Bhagavad Gita and Mahabharata	Related Theories of Resilience	Shlokas/References	Source Reference
Definition of Resilience	Resilience is the ability to endure and recover from crises while maintaining mental and emotional stability.	Psychological Resilience Theory: Resilience as the ability to bounce back from adversity (Masten, 2001).	Gita 2.56: "duḥkheṣv anudvigna-manāḥ sukheṣu vigata-spṛhaḥ" (Stable in distress and detached in joy).	Garg (2019); Pandey & Mishra (2021).
Equanimity in Action	Gita emphasizes acting without attachment to outcomes, achieving resilience through detachment.	Acceptance and Commitment Theory (Hayes et al., 2006): Acceptance of uncontrollable events while maintaining values-driven actions.	Gita 2.38: "sukha-duḥkhe same kṛtvā lābhālābhau jayājayau" (Treat joy and sorrow, gain and loss, victory and defeat alike).	Pandey & Mishra (2021); Garg (2019).

Aspect	Key Insights from Bhagavad Gita and Mahabharata	Related Theories of Resilience	Shlokas/References	Source Reference
Resilience through Letting Go	Characters like Draupadi show resilience by overcoming humiliation and focusing on justice, and Arjuna learns to let go of his doubts.	Cognitive Reframing (Lazarus & Folkman, 1984): Changing the perspective of adversity to grow stronger.	Mahabharata (Bhagavad Gita) 18.62: "tam eva śaraṇaṁ gaccha sarva-bhāvena bhārata" (Surrender to Him with all your heart).	Kumari (2019); Pandey & Mishra (2021).
Resilience through Knowledge	Knowledge (Gyan Yoga) purifies and strengthens resilience by promoting self-awareness and understanding of life's transient nature.	Transformational Coping Theory (Meichenbaum, 1985): Resilience through cognitive restructuring and self-awareness.	Gita 4.38: "na hi jñānena sadṛśaṁ pavitram iha vidyate" (Knowledge is the greatest purifier).	Garg (2019); Pandey & Mishra (2021).

Aspect	Key Insights from Bhagavad Gita and Mahabharata	Related Theories of Resilience	Shlokas/References	Source Reference
Resilience in Adversity	Karna demonstrates resilience by persevering despite societal rejection and maintaining his loyalty to Duryodhana.	Ego-Resilience Theory (Block & Block, 1980): Ability to maintain flexibility and adaptability in adversity.	Mahabharata (Karana Parva): Karna's loyalty to Duryodhana despite learning his true lineage.	Kumari (2019).
Protective Factors	Bhakti Yoga emphasizes devotion and surrender to a higher power, which fosters resilience by providing inner peace and guidance.	Social Support Theory (Beardslee, 1989): Strong relationships enhance resilience.	Gita 12.13-14: "adveṣṭā sarva-bhūtānāṁ maitraḥ karuṇa eva ca" (Compassionate and friendly to all).	Pandey & Mishra (2021); Garg (2019).

CHAPTER 12
Perseverance

Perseverance is a trait that involves persistence and determination in situations of obstacles and challenges. It is different from resilience. Perseverance is a goal-directed persistence in individuals and focused on effort and determination over time. Main triggers of perseverance are challenges and obstacles in goal pursuit and is associated with grit. Resilience is recovery and adaptation from crisis or trauma, emotional and mental recovery. It is a coping ability. The concept is different than perseverance.

Definition of Perseverance

Perseverance is a multifaceted construct and it has been widely researched and defined. One common definition is that it is the ability to persist in pursuit of goals despite obstacles, setbacks or failures (Duckworth et al., 2007).

Perseverance can be defined as a disposition to persist in intellectual/moral endeavours with effort over time, despite obstacles (King, 2014, Baehr 2011). It is a mean between irresolution and intransigence. It can be said that it is rooted in motivation for intellectual and moral goods (Truth, knowledge and understanding). The core conditions for perseverance are effort and seriousness encompassing genuine and sustained engagement with intellectual tasks;

practical wisdom encompassing the timely intervention and overcoming of internal obstacles (fear) and external obstacles (King, 2014; Peterson & Seligman, 2004). Its relationship to other virtues is important to understand. It has been found connected with courage, humility and responsibility. Courage helps in overcoming fears and threats, humility helps avoid intransigence by embracing openness to learning; and responsibility helps in directing perseverance towards a worthy goal. Perseverance is not just persistence over time; it requires effort and the overcoming of genuine obstacles (King, 2014). Overcoming obstacles depends on individual capacity, experience and context (Peterson & Seligman.,2004). Similarly, there are several models for understanding the concept of perseverance in psychology. Agent centric models emphasize motivation, practical wisdom and dynamic adjustment. Contextual models account for systemic and environmental factors in deciding the path of perseverance. Outcome oriented models are focused on intellectual and moral goods but also recognize personal excellence in effort. Obstacles could be divided in the form of internal which include fear, laziness, discouragement. External factors include systemic bias, resource scarcity, and social rejection (King, 2014; Roberts & Wood., 2007; Peterson & Seligman., 2004). The central role of perseverance is that it underpins other virtues by enabling agents to overcome obstacles to intellectual goods (Zagzebski.,1996; King 2014).

Perseverance is a multifaceted construct that has been defined in different ways. One common definition is the ability to persist in the pursuit of goals despite obstacles, setbacks, or failures (Duckworth et al., 2007). Another definition is the sustained effort towards a long-term goal, even when faced with challenges or difficulties (Eisenberg et al., 2005). Regardless of the definition used, perseverance is generally seen as a positive trait that helps individuals achieve success.

Measurement of Perseverance

Measurement of perseverance is a challenging task. Due to its complexity involving multiple facets or dimensions, its measurement has been always a challenging issue. One of the most commonly used scales for measurement of perseverance is the Grit Scale, developed by Duckworth and Colleagues (2007). This scale is based on two dimensions—perseverance of effort and consistency of interests. Volumeter test by Fernald (1912) measures endurance, standing on toes holding dumbbells to measure physical perseverance. Word-building test measures time and number of words formed by Chapman (1924). Downey Will-Temperament Test measures will traits including volitional perseverance. It is made by June Downey (1923). Aggressiveness test by A. R. Gilliland (1926) measures resistance to pain, fatigue and distraction. Motivation persistence from CAQ measure by Christensen and Knezek (2002) measures study habits and persistence in academics.

Academic Perseverance Task Scale developed by Eisenberg et al. (2005) measures the ability to persist in challenging academic tasks. This scale has been used in research widely and has demonstrated good reliability and validity (Eisenberg et al., 2005).

Relationship with Outcomes

In the academic domain, Perseverance has been linked to various outcomes in different fields. In academic field, it has been studied for its linkages with better academic performance, and higher levels of achievement (Duckworth et al., 2007). It has been found that it positively predicts academic achievement across various levels (Chang, 2014; Rimfeld et al., 2016; Jiang et al., 2019; Datu et al., 2017a, 2018a). It also has been associated with increased levels of self-efficacy in general, academic and talent related domains (Jordan et al., 2015; Datu et al., 2017). It is positively related to behavioral cognitive, and emotional engagement in academic settings (Datu et al., 2016, 2018b).

Perseverance has also been linked to various psychological outcomes, such as well-being, resilience, and coping. It promotes intrinsic motivation, goal orientation and mastery over goal orientations (Chen et al., 2018; Datu et al., 2018b). Perseverance predicts higher levels of work performance and reduced burnout (Ceschi et al., 2016; Zhong et al., 2018). It is associated with improved psychological well-being and life satisfaction (Jin & Kim, 2017; Vainio & Daukantaite, 2016). Higher level of perseverance is negatively associated with depression, anxiety, stress in diverse populations (Musumari et al., 2018; Hwang et al., 2018). Its physical benefits in healthier habits, exercise adherence and reduced mental distress are highlighted by scholars (Sharkey et al., 2017; Reed et al., 2013). It improves and sustains attention and neurocognitive functioning related to goal-setting and persistence. Finally, perseverance has been associated with effective coping strategies, such as problem-solving and seeking social support (Wolters & Hussain, 2015).

Factors Affecting Perseverance

Perseverance is influenced by various factors. These include autonomous motivation which have positive effect on perseverance. A significant positive influence of autonomous motivation on perseverance has been observed (Deci & Ryan, 1985; Howard et al., 2021). It is composed of intrinsic motivation, integrated regulation and identified regulation. Perseverance is associated with success in educational and professional contexts (Duckworth et al., 2007).

In addition to academic and professional success, perseverance has been linked to better physical health outcomes. Amotivation or lack of motivation negatively influences perseverance (Vallerand et al., 1997; Calvo et al., 2010). Perseverance should be positively correlated with sense of belonging when studied in isolation but did not show a significant impact in structural model (Carron et al., 1988; Chen & Wang, 2020). Studies have demonstrated the positive impact of perseverance on athletic performance over time (Stoeber et al., 2015).

Despite the numerous benefits of perseverance, there are some negative consequences of excessive perseverance. Over persistence in the face of failure due to any reason may result in anxiety or burnout (Hill et al., 2016). Sometimes, it may lead to inflexibility and stubbornness which may hinder problem-solving and creativity (Luthans et al., 2015). Perseverance and adaptability both are needed for achieving optimal outcomes.

Conclusion:

Perseverance is a complex and multifaceted construct. It has been studied extensively across various domains of academic disciplines and industries. The literature consistently shows it is associated with increased success rate, enhanced mental well-being, academic and professional resilience, better physical health and athletic performance. It is important to find a fit between persistence and adaptability in order to achieve optimal success in life.

Perseverance in Gita

Arjuna's initial reluctance to fight due to inner obstacles (fear and confusion), and Krishna's counsel to persist in his Dharma (Shloka 47, Chapter 2) could be seen as an example of Perseverance. As Perseverance is rooted in motivation for intellectual and moral goods, Krishna's teaching on selfless action and alignment with dharma as the ultimate intellectual and moral pursuit (Shloka 19, Chapter 3; Shloka 47-48, Chapter 2). Effort and seriousness are emphasized in perseverance which can be seen in Krishna emphasizing self-discipline and control of the mind to achieve focus and clarity (Chapter 6, Shlokas 5 & 6). The core conditions for perseverance are overcoming obstacles which is evident in Chapter 18 Shlokas 63-73 where Arjuna overcomes doubt and confusion, and decides to fight for Dharma. If we examine the relationship of perseverance to other values, it can be seen that courage, humility and responsibility are related to perseverance. Krishna encourages Arjuna to act with courage and detachment (Chapter 2, Shloka 37-38). Humility could also be seen in Arjuna's willingness to surrender and learn from Krishna (Chapter 2, Shloka 7). Perseverance requires effort and the overcoming of genuine obstacles, not just persistence. Krishna teaches that effort in disciplined and controlled action leads to liberation, even if immediate success is not achieved (Chapter 6, Shloka 16-17; Chapter 18, Shloka 13-15).

Table 14: Persistence in Srimad Bhagavad Gita

Aspect	**Key Points**	**Examples from the Bhagavad Gita**
Definition	Persistence in intellectual/moral endeavors with effort over time, despite obstacles.	Arjuna's initial reluctance to fight (fear and confusion) and Krishna's counsel to persist in his dharma (2:47).

Aspect	Key Points	Examples from the Bhagavad Gita
First Principle	Rooted in motivation for intellectual and moral goods (truth, knowledge, understanding).	Krishna's teaching on selfless action and alignment with dharma as the ultimate intellectual and moral pursuit (3:19; 2:47-48).
Core Conditions	**Effort and Seriousness**: Genuine, sustained engagement. **Practical Wisdom**: Determines when persistence is appropriate. **Overcoming Obstacles**: Internal (fear, doubt) and external (societal pressures).	Krishna emphasizes self-discipline and control of the mind to achieve focus and clarity (6:5-6). Arjuna overcomes doubt and confusion (18:63-73).
Relationship to Other Virtues	Interacts with courage, humility, and responsibility. **Courage**: Overcomes fears and threats. **Humility**: Embraces openness to learning. **Responsibility**: Directs perseverance toward worthy goals.	Krishna encourages Arjuna to act with courage and detachment (2:37-38). Humility is shown in Arjuna's willingness to surrender and learn from Krishna (2:7).

Aspect	Key Points	Examples from the Bhagavad Gita
Effort vs. Time	Requires effort and overcoming genuine obstacles, not mere persistence.	Krishna teaches that effort in disciplined action leads to liberation, even if immediate success is uncertain (6:16-17; 18:13-15).
Person-Relativity	Obstacles depend on individual capacity, experience, and context (beginner vs. expert challenges).	Krishna tailors his teachings to Arjuna's specific doubts and context, emphasizing personalized dharma (3:35; 18:46-47).
Conditions That Are Not Necessary	Non-epistemic motivations (e.g., personal well-being) can coexist with intellectual aims. Success is not necessary; perseverance is valuable even in failed efforts. Compatible with internal conflicts.	Krishna teaches the importance of action without attachment to the fruits (2:47). Perseverance is shown in striving for perfection even amidst failure (6:40-41).

Aspect	Key Points	Examples from the Bhagavad Gita
Model	**Agent-Centric**: Emphasizes motivation and practical wisdom. **Contextual**: Accounts for environmental factors. **Outcome-Oriented**: Focused on intellectual and moral goods but also recognizes personal excellence in effort.	Krishna's emphasis on yoga (union) integrates self-discipline, self-knowledge, and action toward transcendence, regardless of worldly outcomes (2:50; 3:9).
Obstacles	**Internal**: Fear, laziness, discouragement. **External**: Systemic bias, resource scarcity, social rejection.	Arjuna's despair and fear of killing his kinsmen (1:28-30) are internal obstacles Krishna helps him overcome by providing clarity on dharma and detachment (2:11-13).
Outcome	Leads to epistemic goods (truth, knowledge, understanding) and moral integrity. - Reflects personal excellence even when outcomes fail.	Krishna reveals ultimate knowledge of the Self (Ātman) and the eternal truth (Brahman) as the highest outcomes of perseverance (2:16-18; 15:16-20).

Aspect	Key Points	Examples from the Bhagavad Gita
Central Role	Foundational Virtue: Underpins other virtues by enabling agents to overcome obstacles to intellectual goods.	Krishna underscores perseverance in yoga and selfless action as essential for realizing moksha (liberation) and aligning with one's true self (6:33-36).

Obstacles depend on individual capacity, experience and context so Krishna tailors his teachings to Arjuna's specific doubts and context and explains Dharma as per his condition. Krishna's emphasis on action integrates self-discipline, self-knowledge and action toward transcendence , regardless of worldly outcomes. So Gita proposes an agency-centric motivation and practical wisdom. Major obstacles in perseverance are internal which could be seen in Arjuna's despair and fear of killing his kinsmen (Chapter 1, Shlokas 28-30). Krishna helps him overcome this by providing clarity on Dharma and detachment. As perseverance leads to attainment of epistemic goods, it could be seen that Krishna reveals ultimate knowledge of the self and eternal truth as the highest outcome of perseverance. Foundational virtues underpin other values in perseverance and Krishna underscores perseverance in yoga and selfless action as essential for realization (liberation) and aligning with one's true self (Chapter 6, Shloka 33-36).

In conclusion, the Bhagavad Gita teaches that perseverance is essential for achieving success in all areas of life. By cultivating perseverance, individuals can overcome obstacles; stay focused on their goals, and fulfill their life purpose. Whether it's achieving success in one's career, personal relationships, or spiritual journey, perseverance is a crucial element for achieving success and living a fulfilling life. As Lord Krishna advises Arjuna, "The mind is everything. What you think you become" (Bhagavad Gita 6.5). May we all strive to cultivate perseverance and a positive mindset in our own lives.

Chapter 13
Concept of Authenticity in Gita

Introduction

The Bhagavad Gita is a Hindu scripture that is revered by millions of people worldwide. Krishna teaches Arjuna about being authentic, being a Kshatriya; O Arjuna, fight for the glory, if you win, you will get the whole world; and if you lose, you will be called a righteous Kshatriya. The concept of authenticity in psychology and education is also concerned about developing students with genuine character. Thus, it is necessary to explain the concept clearly. Authenticity is grounded in autonomy or self-authorship, which is the experience of willingly enacting and endorsing one's behaviors, thoughts and decisions. Ryan and Deci (2004; 2017) propose that autonomy refers to a sense of self-authorship without any external coercion or internal conflict. It arises when actions are volitional and aligned with one's values and beliefs without any interference from external control or internalized pressure.

The second component in literature indicates that congruence is important for authenticity. It refers to the alignment between an individual's internal values, feelings and experiences and their outward behavior and expression (Trilling, 1971). Authenticity is about expressing the true self openly and without any distortion (Kernis & Goldman, 2006).

It means that authenticity demands consistency between internal states and external behaviors without any pretense or self-deception.

One more important element of authenticity is genuineness (Relational Openness) which could be defined as interpersonal transparency. This reflects the need for genuine and open engagement with others. It requires the courage to disclose one's true self, particularly in supportive relationships (Reis & Patrick, 1996; Ryan et al., 2012). It adds a social dimension to authenticity by including interpersonal context and dialogue characterized by trust, openness and acceptance.

Psychological perspectives see it from the lens of basic psychological needs (SDT perspective) which highlights that authenticity is intricately tied to the satisfaction of three fundamental needs of autonomy, competence and relatedness (Deci & Ryan, 2000). Supporting environments help in developing authenticity. Self integration and awareness perspectives see it as an integrated form of the self where competing or fragmented identities are reconciled (Sheldon et al., 1997; Weinstein et al., 2017). Mindfulness and self-awareness are necessary for this integration (Brown & Ryan, 2003). This perspective tries to discover the authenticity in the jungle of postmodern fragmented self.

Role of autonomy support is crucial for developing authenticity. Social environments influence authenticity by either supporting autonomy or imposing control. Autonomy supportive relationships require individuals to express their true selves, while controlling environments hinder the expression of true self and thus, suppress authenticity (Legate et al., 2012; Lynch & Sheldon, 2017). So authenticity is situational and fluctuating based on perceived autonomy support in social context.

Authenticity in the Gita

The path to authenticity in the Gita combines overcoming the ego, self-awareness and self-knowledge. It enables individuals to understand their true nature and strengths. By truly understanding true nature of self, an authentic person performs his duties without attachment, interference, or internal conflict. Congruence is required in one's speech and acts and Krishna emphasizes the truthfulness in speech (Shloka 17, Chapter 15). Self-integration is emphasized in Gita which is considered one important characteristics of authenticity. Gita teaches overcoming of ego and recognition of the eternal self beyond physical and mental constructs for holistic integration with the supreme soul. Autonomy support can be seen in support given by Krishna to Arjuna. Dharma is also the greatest autonomy support according to Gita. One who protects the Dharma, Dharma protects him is the central logic in this regard.

Examples of Authenticity in the Gita:

Authenticity is embodied in several characters in Mahabharata and Gita. If we see Yudhishthira, he remains the same in his words and deeds. Even Arjuna on many occasions prepares to die for his oaths. Krishna himself exemplifies authenticity. The genuineness, self-integration, congruence between thought and deed. The entire teaching of Gita is focused on making Arjuna realize his true self and act accordingly.

Krishna's authentic guidance enables Arjuna to understand his own true nature of warrior, and protector of Dharma. Even the Grand Form (Virat Rupa) of Krishna is an example of showing that what he is declaring is true. Krishna finally gives him his Darshana as a God and then Arjuna realizes.

Table 15: Authenticity in the Gita

Dimension	Description	First Principle	Key Citations	Bhagavad Gita Integration	Key Verses/ Citations
Autonomy (Self-Authorship)	Willing enactment of behaviors aligned with personal values and free from coercion.	Authenticity arises when actions are volitional and self-endorsed.	Ryan & Deci (2004; 2017)	Performing duties (dharma) without attachment to results fosters autonomy and aligns actions with higher purpose.	"You are not entitled to the fruits of your actions." (2.47)
Congruence	Alignment between internal values/ experiences and external expressions.	Authenticity requires consistency between inner states and external behaviors.	Sheldon et al. (1997)	Krishna emphasizes the alignment of speech and action with inner truth and kindness, ensuring harmony between values and expressions.	"Speech that is truthful, pleasing, and beneficial is declared as austerity of speech." (17.15)

Dimension	Description	First Principle	Key Citations	Bhagavad Gita Integration	Key Verses/ Citations
Self-Integration	Reconciliation of fragmented identities and fostering self-awareness.	Awareness and integration of values and emotions are prerequisites for authenticity.	Brown & Ryan (2003); Weinstein et al. (2017)	The Gita teaches overcoming ego and recognizing the eternal self beyond physical and mental constructs for holistic integration.	"The wise see action in inaction, and inaction in action." (4.18)
Autonomy Support	Influence of autonomy-supportive relationships in facilitating authenticity.	Social contexts that support autonomy encourage self-expression and reduce suppression.	Legate et al. (2012)	Krishna's autonomy-supportive approach encourages Arjuna to embrace his dharma authentically without coercion or fear.	"Better to strive in one's own dharma than to succeed in the dharma of another." (18.47)

Dimension	Description	First Principle	Key Citations	Bhagavad Gita Integration	Key Verses/ Citations
Dynamic Nature	Variability of authenticity across roles, relationships, and contexts.	Authenticity is a dynamic state shaped by situational autonomy and relational trust.	Sheldon et al. (1997); Lynch et al. (2004)	Arjuna's authenticity varies across contexts (e.g., family loyalty vs. warrior duty); Krishna guides him to integrate his roles dynamically through detachment and dharma.	"The wise person who is free from doubt acts in harmony with their duties." (4.41)
Costs and Courage	Balancing risks of rejection with the need for authentic self-expression.	Authenticity requires courage to maintain self-expression despite social risks.	Kierkegaard (1849); Yalom (1980)	Arjuna's courage to follow his dharma despite personal loss and societal judgment exemplifies the risk and resilience of authenticity.	"One's own dharma, though imperfect, is better than the dharma of another well-performed." (3.35)

Dimension	Description	First Principle	Key Citations	Bhagavad Gita Integration	Key Verses/ Citations
Well-Being Connection	Association of authenticity with psychological and relational health.	Authenticity promotes well-being, while inauthenticity undermines mental health and vitality.	Kernis (2003); Ryan et al. (2005)	Authentic living through dharma leads to spiritual liberation (moksha), mental clarity, and harmony, aligning with psychological well-being.	"When a man lets go of all desires and lives free from longing and ego, he finds peace." (2.71)

He apologize that "I didn't understand you and have called you friend, O Lord Forgive Me". The authenticity is one of the core methods of Krishna to awaken Arjuna. Krishna's guidance to Arjuna is based on his deep understanding of the nature of reality, and his advice is rooted in self-knowledge and detachment.

Challenges to Authenticity in the Gita

The Gita recognizes that there are several challenges to authenticity, including societal and cultural expectations, desires, and attachments. Authenticity is especially challenged in stigmatized or devaluing environments. For individuals with concealable stigmatized identities such as transgender individuals, LGB persons, or persons with deformed bodies; autonomy-supportive contexts are crucial for fostering openness and self-expression (Ryan et al., 2017; Weinstein et al., 2012). When acceptance and autonomy support from the environment exceeds rejection or judgment, authenticity is encouraged. Authenticity varies across contexts and relationships, and is influenced by situational factors such as supportive environment and relational trust (Sheldon et al., 1997). It can be said that authenticity is both a disposition and a dynamic state shaped by internal and external factors. Authentic individuals have been found having higher well-being, greater vitality, and stronger relational bonds (Ryan and Deci, 2017; Kernis, 2003). It promotes psychological and relational health and its absence leads to fragmentation.

Application in Educational Psychology and Teaching Learning

The concept of authenticity in the Gita has several applications in educational psychology and teaching and learning. Authenticity can be applied in several areas, including student motivation, teacher-student relationships, and student well-being. It emphasizes the importance of autonomy in students by allowing choice and encouraging self-directed learning aligned with values. Promotes congruence by encouraging students to reflect on their beliefs and ensure alignment with their actions and expressions. It can support self-awareness and mindfulness practices to help students integrate fragmented identities and reconcile conflicts. Autonomy support is needed for creating supportive environments where teachers mentor students, encourage them for self-expression without undue pressure.

Finally, authenticity can contribute to student well-being by promoting resilience and risk-taking in expressing authentic ideas, even in the face of peer pressure. Authentic living leads to mental clarity, harmony and spiritual liberation. It highlights the link between authenticity and well-being promoting a classroom culture that values genuine self-expression.

Conclusion

In conclusion, it can be said that authenticity is a critical concept in the Gita. It stresses the essentiality of spiritual growth and personal development. Authenticity involves being true to oneself and genuine expression of self. The uncoordinated living where there is a difference between speech and act creates a mental haze. This mental unclarity hinders the genuine process of knowing and understanding the true self. By promoting autonomy, congruence and self-integration authenticity in Gita prepares individuals who are capable of understanding their true self, its eternal nature and prepare for selfless duties with an enhanced mental being, mental clarity without any kind of confusion and conflict.

It has several implications in educational psychology including student motivation, teacher student relationship, fostering a culture supportive of autonomy and self-expression. Thus, the concept of authenticity in Gita provides a framework to understand the personal growth and development and can contribute to student success and well-being.

Chapter 14
Self-transcendence in Gita

Self-transcendence implies transcending individual boundaries of self-centeredness to altruism, spiritual awareness and purpose. It connects an individual with broader existential or universal dimension (Cloninger, 2004; Erikson, 1982; Frankl, 1963; Maslow, 1971; Piedmont, 1999). Further, it can be said that it involves going beyond self-interest, to embrace a connection with the larger whole. It is derived from developmental psychology, existential logotherapy and personality theory (Cloninger, 2004; Erikson, 1982; Frankl, 1963; Maslow, 1971; Reed, 1991; Tornstam, 1999). It includes acceptance, spiritual/universal connectedness, and altruism (Garcia et al., 2014; Kabat-Zinn, 1990; Levenson et al., 2005; Piedmont, 1999; Reed, 1991). Its psychological impact includes resilience, life satisfaction, and reduced distress through meaning and mindfulness (Garcia et al., 2014; Kabat-Zinn, 1990; Morgan & Farsides, 2009; Piedmont, 1999). Three dimensions are given by Tornstam (1999) which are expansion of boundaries, integration with the whole and awareness of transience. Maslow's hierarchy of needs theory highlights that self-transcendence extends beyond self-actualization, fostering meaning and contribution to the world (Maslow, 1971). Cloninger's model describes self-transcendence as a character dimension which reflects spirituality and connectedness

(Cloninger., 2004). According to Erickson ego transcendence emerges in later stages which aligns finite existence with a sense of legacy (Erickson, 1982). Self-transcendence helps in resilience and coping by meaning making strategies enhance resilience during adversity. Life satisfaction is another impact. It establishes connection to existential dimensions correlated

Table 16: Self-transcendence Theory Summary

Section	Key Points	In-text Citations
Introduction	Self-transcendence involves transcending individual boundaries to connect with broader existential or universal dimensions.	Reed (1991); Cloninger (2004)
	Represents a shift from self-centeredness to altruism, spiritual awareness, and purpose.	Levenson et al. (2005)
Definition	Involves going beyond self-interest to embrace a connection with the larger whole.	Cloninger (2004); Maslow (1971)
	Three dimensions: Expansion of boundaries, integration with the whole, and awareness of transience.	Tornstam (1999)

Section	Key Points	In-text Citations
Theoretical Foundations	Maslow's Hierarchy of Needs: Self-transcendence extends beyond self-actualization, fostering meaning and contribution to the world.	Maslow (1971)
	Cloninger's Model: Describes self-transcendence as a character dimension reflecting spirituality and connectedness.	Cloninger (2004)
	Erikson's Stages: Ego transcendence emerges in later stages, aligning finite existence with a sense of legacy.	Erikson (1982)
Characteristics & Dimensions	Spiritual Awareness: Heightened sense of connection with universal principles.	Piedmont (1999)
	Altruism & Compassion: Dedication to serving others and addressing societal concerns.	Reed (1991)
	Existential Awareness: Acceptance of mortality fosters meaningful living.	Frankl (1963)

Section	Key Points	In-text Citations
	Openness to Experience: Willingness to explore new perspectives and embrace uncertainty.	Garcia et al. (2014)
Impact on Well-being	Resilience & Coping: Meaning-making strategies enhance resilience during adversity.	Morgan & Farsides (2009)
	Life Satisfaction: Connection to existential dimensions correlates with increased satisfaction and reduced distress.	Levenson et al. (2005)
	Reduction of Egoic Suffering: Reduces isolation and dissatisfaction by diminishing self-centered thinking.	Tornstam (1999)
Pathways to Self-Transcendence	Mindfulness & Meditation: Foster present-moment awareness and reduce ego-driven thought patterns.	Kabat-Zinn (1990)
	Altruistic Activities: Service to others fosters connection and purpose.	Reed (1991)

Section	Key Points	In-text Citations
	Reflection on Mortality: Contemplating impermanence encourages focus on enduring values.	Frankl (1963)
	Peak/Flow Experiences: Intense harmony with the environment transcends self-boundaries.	Maslow (1971)
Applications	Mental Health: Logotherapy and mindfulness-based therapies integrate self-transcendence principles to promote meaning and reduce distress.	Frankl (1963); Kabat-Zinn (1990)
	Education: Encouraging connection between learning and existential questions fosters purpose and broadens thinking.	Reed (1991)
	Community Development: Promoting self-transcendent values enhances collective well-being and social cohesion.	Cloninger (2004)

Section	Key Points	In-text Citations
Conclusion	Self-transcendence fosters personal growth and societal harmony by encouraging connections beyond individual concerns.	Reed (1991); Cloninger (2004)
	Practices like mindfulness, altruism, and reflection can cultivate self-transcendence, enriching lives and fostering a compassionate world.	Maslow (1971); Frankl (1963); Kabat-Zinn (1990)

Pathways to self-transcendence includes mindfulness and meditation which means fostering present-moment awareness and reduce ego-driven thought patterns, altruistic activities (service to others fosters connection and purpose), reflection on morality (Contemplating impermanence encourages focus on enduring values. Harmony with the environment transcends self-boundaries. Its applications in psychology and education are various. In the area of mental health, logotherapy and mindfulness-based therapies integrate self-transcendence principles to promote meaning and reduce distress. In education encouraging connection between learning and existential questions fosters purpose and broadens thinking. Promoting self-transcendent enhances collective well-being and social cohesion. (Cloninger, 2004; Kabat-Zinn, 1990; Reed, 1991; Tornstam, 1999)

Self-transcendence in Gita

In Gita, transcending egoic concerns to connect with universal moral principles and divine will is self-transcendence. It is implemented through the mechanisms of karma yoga- the path of selfless action as devotion to the divine, Bhakti Yoga, surrendering and paying devotion to Krishna; and Gyan Yoga realization of unity with universal or Brahman through knowledge.

Table 17 : Self-transcendence in Gita

Aspect	Conceptualization in the Bhagavad Gita	Supporting Citations
Definition	Transcending egoic concerns to connect with universal principles, divine will, and spiritual purpose.	Bhagavad Gita (2.20; 2.50); Cloninger (2004); Maslow (1971)
Theoretical Basis	**Karma Yoga:** Path of selfless action as devotion to the divine. **Bhakti Yoga:** Surrender and devotion to Krishna. **Jnana Yoga:** Realization of unity with Brahman through knowledge. **Raja Yoga:** Meditation to achieve spiritual insight.	Bhagavad Gita (3.7-9; 6.20-23; 9.22); Radhakrishnan (1929); Feuerstein (1974)

Aspect	Conceptualization in the Bhagavad Gita	Supporting Citations
Key Characteristics	**Selflessness:** Acting without attachment to results. **Universal Connectedness:** Recognition of unity in all beings. **Emotional Regulation:** Detachment from fear, anger, and desire. **Equanimity:** Even-mindedness in success and failure.	Bhagavad Gita (2.47; 2.64-65; 5.10); Tornstam (1999); Levenson et al. (2005)
Dimensions	**Spiritual Awareness:** Realizing the eternal nature of the self (Atman). **Integration with Whole:** Serving the universal purpose. **Awareness of Transience:** Accepting impermanence while focusing on higher goals.	Bhagavad Gita (13.27-28; 6.29-30); Tornstam (1999); Erikson (1982)

Aspect	Conceptualization in the Bhagavad Gita	Supporting Citations
Psychological Impacts	**Enhanced Resilience:** Meaning-making helps face adversity. **Life Satisfaction:** Connection to existential purpose. **Reduction of Suffering:** Diminished ego-driven dissatisfaction.	Bhagavad Gita (2.14-15; 2.70-71); Maslow (1971); Garcia et al. (2014); Morgan & Farsides (2009)
Pathways	**Mindfulness:** Cultivation of awareness through meditation and yoga. **Altruism:** Serving others with devotion. **Reflection on Mortality:** Understanding impermanence inspires alignment with higher values. **Devotion:** Worship and surrender to Krishna.	Bhagavad Gita (6.5-7; 11.54; 12.6-8); Kabat-Zinn (1990); Frankl (1963); Maslow (1971)

Aspect	Conceptualization in the Bhagavad Gita	Supporting Citations
Applications	**Mental Health:** Incorporating meaning-making and mindfulness in therapy. **Education:** Linking learning to existential questions. **Community Development:** Promoting selfless action for collective well-being.	Bhagavad Gita (18.66); Frankl (1963); Kabat-Zinn (1990); Cloninger (2004)
Universal Connections	Encourages seeing the divine presence in all beings and acting without ego to uphold cosmic harmony.	Bhagavad Gita (10.20; 11.9-19); Reed (1991); Piedmont (1999)
Core Teachings on Equanimity	Detachment from outcomes. Balanced response to pleasure and pain. Awareness of impermanence.	Bhagavad Gita (2.14; 2.48; 6.15); Maslow (1971); Tornstam (1999)
Symbolic Representation	Krishna as the eternal guide, reflecting divine wisdom and universal truths.	Bhagavad Gita (11.13-15; 18.66); Radhakrishnan (1929); Erikson (1982)

It can be said that self-transcendence fosters personal and societal harmony by encouraging connections beyond individual concerns. Mindfulness practice, altruism and reflection can cultivate self-transcendence, enriching lives and fostering a compassionate world.

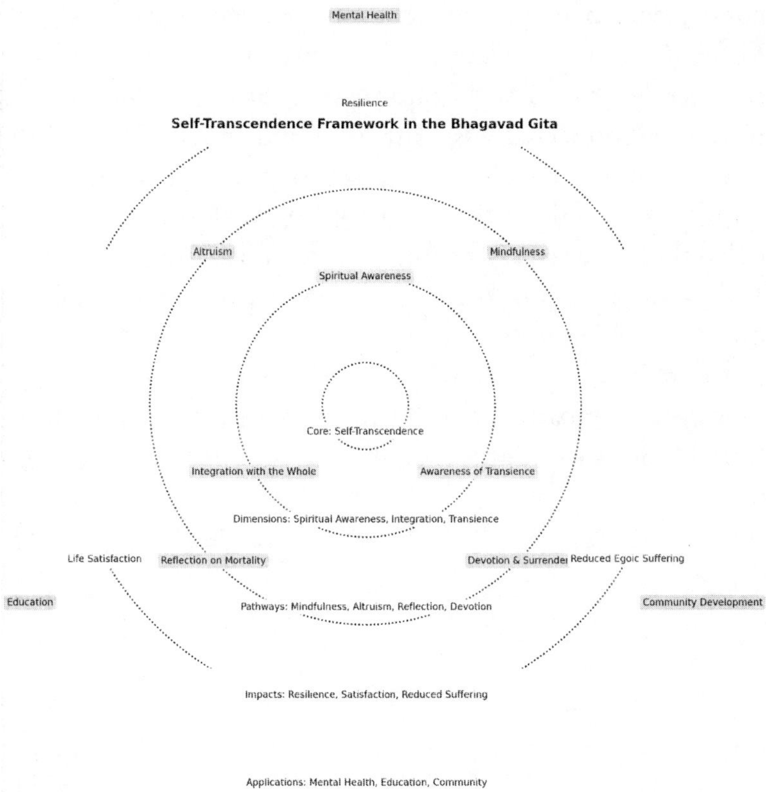

Key charecteristics include selflessness, acting without attachment to results and anxiety; universal connectedness (Recognition of unity in all beings) and equanimity in success and failure. Gita provides a view which supports that spiritual awareness, integration with the whole and awareness of transience are main dimensions of self-transcendence. Spiritual awareness is about realizing the eternal nature of the self. Integration with whole ensures that individual serves universal purpose of being human. Awareness of transience is awareness about transient and impermanent nature of the worldly affairs, while focusing on higher purpose.

The diagram presents self-transcendence as the core concept which involves going beyond self-centered boundaries. It provides an overview of theoretical foundations of self-transcendence in Gita. The first layer is made of self-awareness, universal connectedness, altruism and duty. The second layer shows the pathways to self-transcendence including mindfulness and meditation (Raj Yoga), devotion and love (Bhakti Yoga), selfless action (Karma Yoga) and Knowledge and Wisdom (Jnana Yoga). Outer layer presents the impacts on psychological well-being including resilience, inner peace, reduced egoic suffering and life satisfaction. Feedback loops indicate pathways influence well-being and theoretical foundations shape pathways.

CHAPTER 15
The Mind-body Connection in Gita

The mind-body connection is a concept that has been discussed for centuries in western and eastern philosophical discourses. It refers to the relationship between mental and physical states and the mechanisms by which they affect each other and work in coordination. Thus mind-body connection is a fundamental part of understanding human behavior, well-being and health. In the discipline of psychology, mind-body connection is studied in the context of stress and its regulation and influence on the body. Stress is treated as an evidence of connection between the mind and the body.

According to the biopsychosocial model of health, all three factors — biological, psychological and social factors influence the health of the individual. The model suggests the interdependence of these three; indicating that all three can affect each other. Physical and bodily related issues can influence the social and psychological behavior of the person and similarly social and psychological factors can influence the physical well-being of the person. Stress can cause physical symptoms such as headaches, stomachaches, memory loss, abnormal behavior and maladjustment in social contexts.

One of the most well-known examples of the mind-body connection is the placebo effect which is experienced by a person experiencing change in their physical symptoms after taking a treatment that is inert. This change occurs due to the belief that the drug is actually working and the body's natural healing processes are activated.

The empirical evidence from mindfulness research indicates that it is useful in reducing stress and improving mental health. Mindfulness meditation involves paying attention to the present moment and awareness of the physical and mental states of a person without any judgement. It has been shown to be linked with a variety of health benefits — reducing stress, improving mood and reducing symptoms of depression and anxiety in individuals.

The mind-body connection can also be seen in the fact that persons with stress and mental illness have greater chances of getting ill or having conditions of heart disease, respiration and asthmatic symptoms. This indicates that mental health can affect the physical well-being and biological processes of a person.

In addition to the evidence about impact of mental health on physical health, the mind-body connection can also be seen in the relationship between physical health and mental health. Chronic pain in a person can lead to depression and anxiety, and chronic illness such as cancer can have a significant impact on a person's mental health and psychological well-being. Thus, it can be said that the mind-body connection is a complex and important concept in psychology highlighting the interplay between psychological and physical well-being. Understanding the mind-body connection is necessary for the promotion of health and well-being. It has important implications for the treatment of physical and mental health conditions.

The mind-body connection is a concept that has been studied from the perspective of ancient philosophical and theological perspectives. In the Bhagavad Gita, it is explored in holistic perspective. The mind serves as a mediator between the body and the metaphysical self or Atman. Balance in the physical body directly influences mental well-being and spiritual clarity and practices like yoga, meditation, and Ayurveda emphasize the connection, offering holistic solutions for health and self-realization. Understanding of the mind-body connection from the perspective of the Gita and its relevance to modern educators can promote holistic approaches to education that addresses the physical, emotional, and social needs of students.

Karma yoga is one of the key concepts in Gita's teachings about the mind-body connection which emphasizes selfless and detached work for peaceful living. The detachment from the fruits of one's actions enables a person to focus on the process of action rather than the outcome. It could be said that Gita promotes process-centered approach, where everything has to be done according to the desired Dharma. Focusing on process requires mind-body connection and integration of psychomotor abilities. It demands for a harmonious relationship between the mind and the body for attaining spiritual goals.

Another important concept in the Gita's teaching about the mind-body connection is the three eternal gunas—Satva, Rajas, and Tamas. This resonates with Sankhya philosophy. These qualities are present in the whole creation. Mind and body are just deformation of Prakriti, which is composed of a balance of three gunas. Mind is the mediator between soul and body. Self-control includes control of senses and mind. It is emphasized in Gita that elevation and control of mind toward higher causes is necessary for raising the consciousness. A controlled mind is the best friend and an uncontrolled mind is the worst enemy of a person (Shloka 5, Chapter 6). Yoga or discipline is highlighted as a medium to control mind and body. Disciplined lifestyle and eating habits are emphasized in Chapter 6, shloka 16 as interplay between mental and physical states.

Yoga is also presented as a medium of achieving a state of self-realization or Moksha which helps in achieving deep sense of inner peace and connection to the cosmos and super consciousness. Through the practice of yoga, one can achieve control of his senses and mind and understand that detachment is the way to achieve inner peace. The greater mental clarity achieved through yoga and discipline helps in maintaining a harmonious relationship between the mind and body.

The Relevance of the Mind-Body Connection in Modern Psychology

The concepts of the mind-body connection in the Bhagavad Gita provide several insights for modern psychology and philosophy. Research has shown that mental health affects physical health. Mindfulness and yoga can enhance physical health and well-being. Yoga has shown a variety of physical and mental health benefits and studies have concluded that it can reduce stress and enhance cardiovascular health outcomes, as well as overall well-being (Ross et al., 2010). Mindfulness can be useful in reducing symptoms of anxiety and depression and can improve cognitive and affective functioning. It can also enhance emotional regulation (Hofmann et al., 2010).

Implications for Educational Psychology

The teachings of the Bhagavad Gita on the mind-body connection have important insights for educational psychology. By understanding the relationship between body and mind, students can be encouraged to learn self-discipline and deal with anxiety and motivational problems with the principles of Karma Yoga and detachment. The fundamental essence which is applicable in the Gita is emphasis on good character. Gita metaphorically defines body as a field and emphasizes the need of developing good habits as seeds in the character and body.

CHAPTER 16
Self-compassion in Gita

Introduction

Self-compassion has gained increased attention in contemporary psychology due to its importance in maintaining a coherent self and promotes well-being, resilience, and overall health (Neff, 2011). Self-compassion is also an important aspect of Hinduism because it allows individuals to develop self-awareness, a righteous path, detachment and acceptance of one's own limitations. Accepting one's own limitations is critical for accepting oneself, and it helps in reducing the tension between the imaginations and expectations of a person's distorted self and actual self. By avoiding this imaginary tension and the maladjustment created by them in real life, one can really help himself be more integrated, reality-oriented and task-oriented. The orientation of karma requires a true understanding of oneself. Actually, self-compassion relates to the concept of knowing one's own Dharma and nature—which is made of three Gunas—Satva, Rajas, and Tamas. If a person knows his nature and Dharma, he can be truly compassionate to himself or herself. Without knowing own nature, duty, and limitations one cannot do justice to himself. Throughout the Gita, Krishna teaches Arjuna about the nature of reality, self, the importance of dharma (duty), and the path to liberation.

The Importance of Self-Compassion in the Bhagavad Gita

The concept of self-compassion is implied in the Gita's teachings about the nature of the self, worldly affairs, and the Supreme Divine. The self (Atman) is real, eternal and indestructible. It is also a part of larger divine reality Brahman, which pervades all existence of living and non-living beings in the universe. Thus, knowing oneself is all about accepting that the soul of the individual is not going to die, but a born person has suffering if he doesn't act according to his Dharma. So, knowing the Dharma is the first step. That is Gyan Yoga. Karm Yoga moves towards action. A person who knows himself, the indestructible soul, has control over the senses and mind, knows his true nature and balance of Gunas, his personality can take care of his own self and personality. The Gita encourages individuals to cultivate a sense of self-compassion by recognizing the fundamental worth and dignity of the self, which is not dependent on external circumstances or achievements.

Krishna also emphasizes the importance of non-attachment. The principle of non-attachment is fundamental to the concept of self-compassion. An attached person will get anger, get frustration and get suffering and this will interfere in the process of righteous conduct. Deviation from righteous conduct creates tension, either in the form of internal and moral conflict or external and societal pressure. Thus, Krisna advises Arjuna to perform his duty. The true care of self is to adhere to the duties for larger society. Dharma is for preservation and maintenance of society. Thus, Gita encourages individuals to develop a sense of detachment from their own ego-driven desires and fears, which can lead to greater self-acceptance and compassion.

Cultivating Self-Compassion in the Bhagavad Gita

Gita offers several practical ways to understand the self and compassion towards it. Without understanding the self, one can't care for it. Self-awareness and mindfulness are important to self-compassion. It needs reflecting about oneself in a non-judgmental way, observing one's own thoughts, emotions and behaviors. Krishna advises Arjuna to be steadfast in yoga. To be consistent in controlling the senses, taking them apart from their subjects of distraction which is the root cause of desire. Desire creates expectation and when expectation is not met, frustration and anger are created. The creation of anger leads to loss of memory or loss of righteous conduct which becomes the cause of very suffering or destruction of the person. This advice highlights the importance of developing mindfulness and non-judgmental awareness which leads to greater self-compassion.

Another technique for cultivating self-compassion in the Gita is the practice of self-inquiry. *Uddharet Atmana Atmanam* (Chapter 6, Shloka 5). Western philosophy is full of the similar queries – *Know Thyself, Who Am I, I think therefore I am.* This practice can help individuals in differentiating the transient nature of their personalities and circumstances. This would enable them to understand their true unchanging self, fostering greater self-acceptance and compassion.

The Gita also emphasizes the importance of guidance of experienced and competent person, which seems closer to the principle of learning of scaffolding (Vygotsky,..). Arjuna sought help from Krishna to achieve and understand reality. It is necessary for cultivating self-compassion and to achieve spiritual growth. Krishna advises Arjuna to seek the guidance of a wise teacher who can help him to overcome his doubts and fears. Until a competent guidance is received one can't achieve a deeper understanding of the nature of the self and the divine (Gita Chapter 4, Shloka 31).

The Relevance of Self-Compassion in the Bhagavad Gita for Contemporary Educational Psychology

The Gita's teachings on self-compassion provide critical insights for contemporary psychology and educational perspectives. In the area of mindfulness-based interventions, research has shown that they can improve self-compassion and reduce symptoms of anxiety, depression and stress (Neff & Germer, 2013). Self-compassion can help in the enhancement of academic performance by reducing anxiety, depression, and stress and strengthening cognitive functions and building resilience. It has been found that it encourages kinder self-talk and helps individuals recover from mistakes more effectively (Bluth & Blanton, 2015; Hope, Koestner & Milyavskaya, 2014; Iranzo-Bennett, Egan, Cook & Mantzios, 2018; Keyes, Shmotkin & Ryff, 2002; Neff, 2003a, 2003b; Ryan & Deci, 2000; Ryff, 1989a, 1995). This research support Gita's emphasis on the development of mindfulness-based interventions that incorporate spiritual practices.

Furthermore, the Gita's teachings on the importance of seeking guidance from wise and experienced counsel like Krishna can inform psychotherapy practices. It can help integrate self-compassion techniques into curricula that can encourage students to handle academic setbacks more constructively. Psychologically, self-compassion enhances adaptive emotion regulation, and helps reduce diminishing self-criticism (Bakosh, Snow, Tobias, Houlihan & Barbosa-Leiker, 2016; Egan et al., 2018; Neff, Kirkpatrick & Rude, 2007; Sirois, 2014). The Gita's emphasis on the role of the guru as a wise and compassionate guide can provide a model for the development of therapeutic relationships that promote self-compassion and spiritual growth.

Conclusion

Self-compassion is an important aspect of spiritual growth in Gita and general philosophical orientation of Hinduism. Through the cultivation of self-awareness, individuals can develop greater self-compassion towards themselves and acceptance of own limitations. Mindfulness based interventions can enhance the overall well-being. It has been found that factors like parental education and supportive family environments influence adolescents self-compassion and can guide educational policies toward family and community engagement . Self-compassion interacts with personality traits like extroversion, and openness, influencing self-acceptance, personal growth and emotional staibility (Grant, Langan-Fox & Anglim, 2009; Neff, 2003a, 2003b; Sarıcaoğlu & Arslan, 2013; Schmutte & Ryff, 1997). Thus development of mindfulness-based interventions and psychotherapy practices promotes self-compassion and spiritual growth.

CHAPTER 17
Self-acceptance in Gita

Self-acceptance is a crucial aspect of personal growth and well-being, which involves acknowledging and embracing one's true self, including one's strengths, weaknesses, and imperfections. Acknowledge and embrace oneself as inherently valuable including one's thoughts, weaknesses and strengths. It includes viewing oneself with compassion and non-judgemental awareness is important (Bernard, 2013; Dryden & Still, 2006; Shepard, 1979). Core theoretical foundations are rooted in humanistic psychology, which emphasizes authenticity, creativity and fulfilment of human potential (Bernard., 2013; Dryden and Still, 2006).

Table 18 : Self-acceptance in Gita

Theme	Description and Insights	Citations
Definition of Self-Acceptance	— Acknowledging and embracing oneself as inherently valuable, including one's strengths and weaknesses. — Viewing oneself with compassion and nonjudgmental awareness.	Bernard (2013), Dryden & Still (2006), Shepard (1979)

Theme	Description and Insights	Citations
Core Theoretical Foundations	— Rooted in humanistic psychology, emphasizing authenticity, creativity, and fulfillment of human potential. — Influenced by mindfulness practices integrating Eastern philosophies and Western psychology.	Bernard (2013), Dryden & Still (2006)
Relationship to Self-Actualization	— Humanistic psychologists (Maslow, Rogers) place self-acceptance as a key milestone in the self-actualization process, highlighting its dynamic and ongoing nature. — Actualization involves awareness, discovery, and integration of the self.	Bernard (2013), Shepard (1979)
Interpersonal Dynamics	— Self-acceptance improves interpersonal relationships by fostering openness and understanding toward others. — Accepting oneself enhances empathy and nonjudgmental acceptance of others' experiences.	Bernard (2013), Dryden & Still (2006), Crowne & Marlowe (1961)

Theme	Description and Insights	Citations
Role of Vulnerability	— Acknowledging limitations, imperfections, and "negative" traits allows individuals to face themselves honestly. — Vulnerability is essential for authentic self-growth and meaningful connections.	Bernard (2013), Dryden & Still (2006)
Therapeutic Implications	— Humanistic therapy uses self-acceptance as a foundational goal for healing and growth. — Mindfulness-based interventions (like Kabat-Zinn's MBSR) emphasize nonjudgmental acceptance of self and experiences. — Therapists must also embrace their own vulnerabilities to guide clients effectively.	Bernard (2013), Dryden & Still (2006), Shepard (1979)
Psychological Constructs	— Related to self-esteem and authenticity in behavior, but distinct from them in its focus on nonjudgmental self-awareness. — Crowne and Marlowe explore the social desirability bias in measuring self-acceptance.	Crowne & Marlowe (1961), Shepard (1979)

Theme	Description and Insights	Citations
Mindfulness Perspective	— Defined as a balanced evaluation of one's identity and experiences, integrating the practice of mindfulness to achieve nonjudgmental awareness. — Encourages living in the present moment with clarity.	Dryden & Still (2006), Bernard (2013)
Cultural Perspectives	— Zhi Mian, from Chinese existential traditions, emphasizes "facing life directly" as a pathway to authentic self-acceptance. — Integrating cultural and philosophical ideas enriches Western therapeutic approaches.	Bernard (2013), Dryden & Still (2006)
Complexities and Challenges	— Self-acceptance is not a one-time achievement but an ongoing process requiring continuous adaptation. — Accepting destructive tendencies (May's daimonic) or past failures fosters holistic self-awareness.	Bernard (2013), Shepard (1979), Crowne & Marlowe (1961)

Theme	Description and Insights	Citations
Everyday Relevance	— Maslow highlights "everyday creativity" as a component of self-acceptance, where mundane tasks and humour express self-actualization. — Accepting oneself impacts decision-making, relationships, and life satisfaction.	Bernard (2013), Shepard (1979)

The Bhagavad Gita is a sacred text of Hinduism containing profound wisdom on this aspect. The core theoretical foundations are rooted in humanistic psychology and emphasizes authenticity, creativity, and fulfillment of human potential. Mindfulness practices seem to integrate eastern philosophies and western psychology (Bernard, 2013; Dryden & Still, 2006). The Gita teaches that self-acceptance is a vital part of the path of spiritual enlightenment which involves understanding and accepting the true nature of the self and one's relationship with the universe. The teaching of the Gita promotes a holistic approach to self-acceptance which encompasses the physical, mental, emotional and spiritual dimensions of the self (Easwaran, 2007).

The Gita presents several key verses that emphasize the importance of self-acceptance. For example, in Chapter 2, Shloka 56, it states, "unattached to the fruits of his work, a person achieves perfection in his Karma and works according to his prescribed duties of Dharma which is the renounced order of life. This verse highlights the importance of detachment from the outcomes of one's actions and the acceptance of one's obligations in life. In Chapter 12, verse 13 of Gita, it is said that who is equal to friends and enemies and equipoised in honor and dishonor and odd conditions; name and fame can lead to liberation. This emphasis on remaining free from contaminating association of senses is about being self-compassionate. Self-compassion involves taking care of one's self as a spiritual being tied to the social duties and social self. The self of the individual is a part of universal self spiritually and theories of collective consciousness indicate that major part of self is constructed by social influence and interactions. This alignment between self and universal and social self of present social psychology, indicates that a person needs to abide by the social self by following desired social duties. Any deviation may create a state of internal conflict. This internal conflict and suffering can be reduced by following equanimity and acceptance of all aspects of life, without being affected by external circumstances.

Furthermore, the Gita presents the unique concept of surrendering your ego to the supreme. Ego is seen as a false accumulation of self-image based on unreal possession, and non-prescribed karma. Krisna at one place says that you surrender to me and I shall take care of your all business. Surrender to me and do the prescribed duty, if you lose you will stay in your Dharma and will be called righteous; if you win you will acquire the earth; so you do not fear. This verse highlights the importance of sacrificing ego and placing trust in the higher power to overcome obstacles and achieve true inner peace.

In addition to this, the Gita also highlights the importance of detachment which needs letting go the attachment to material possessions, sensual desires, physical achievements and relationships. In Chapter 6, Shloka 35, it is said that " the supreme state of detachment is achieved by disciplining the mind and body for achieving spiritual liberation and inner peace. The Gita also presents the concept of eternal self which is unchanging and universal essence of the individual. It is beyond the temporary and changing aspects of the body, mind and emotions and cherished highly in Gita. The self is eternally divine and accepting it needs recognition and embracement of this divine essence within oneself (Easwaran, 2007).

Self-acceptance has numerous benefits for personal growth and well-being. Humanist psychologists such as, Maslow, Rogers found that self-acceptance is a key milestone in the self-actualization process. It highlights the dynamic and ongoing nature of self. Self-actualization involves awareness, discovery and integration of the self. self-acceptance fosters greater authenticity, self-expression and personal growth allowing individuals to live more fulfilling, integrated and meaningful lives. It provides insights for interpersonal dynamics by advocating openness and understanding toward others. Accepting oneself enhances empathy and non-judgemental acceptance of others' experiences. The Gita's core teachings about self-acceptance are based on the principles of equanimity in odd situations and favourable situations, detachment and surrender to higher authority of Krishna or Dharma. Thus, these principles encourage individuals to cultivate a sense of inner peace and acceptance of their true selves, regardless of external circumstances.

One of the key verses in the Gita that highlights the importance of self-acceptance is Chapter 2, Shloka 56 which highlights that the unattachment to the results of the action and is according to the order of prescribed Dharma as the renounced order of life is the true way of Yogi. It is not necessary to light fire and doing rituals. This necessitates the importance of working as per the standard operating procedures in corporate life and in social life as per Dharma. In other words, the Gita teaches that self-acceptance brings a person to the level of actual reality and helps in overcoming false ego. It is important to Control ego, recognize one's limitations, and also working towards one's goals without becoming overly attached to the results.

Another key principle of self-acceptance in the Gita is the concept of surrendering oneself to the supreme. Surrender to god or supreme involves sacrificing desires and physical ambitions. In Chapter 12, Shloka 13 the Gita states, "equanimity in friendship and enmity, honour and dishonour, heat and cold, happiness and distress, fame and infamy, who is always free from contaminating association is true Yogi and realized person. By surrendering ego and desires and expectations this type of person achieves inner peace and true happiness.

Moreover, detachment plays also an important role in self-acceptance in the Gita. A person with overambitions and insatiable desires cannot achieve true peace. The supreme state of detachment is attained by practicing self-restrain, discipline and Yoga (Chapter 6, Shloka 35). Thus Gita highlights the importance of detachment as a means to achieve spiritual liberation and inner peace.

The Gita's teachings on self-acceptance are related to the concept of self in it. The true Self in Gita is immortal, unchangeable, soul and part of the supreme soul, Krishna. This integration with cosmos serves at least two purposes — first to propose a sense of connection with all human living and non-living beings in the cosmos, and Second; to overcome the sense of bodily ego or an impermanent and highly changeable aura which is not eternal but seems to be true. This could be achieved by understanding the true knowledge of the real nature of the self and overcoming the tensions caused by false egoism. In Chapter 2, Verse 23, the Gita states "The soul cannot be burnt by fire, nor moistened by water, nor withered by the wind and cannot be pierced by sword." Self is a transcendent, immortal entity beyond the realm of material world.

Furthermore, to understand the nature of self, self-knowledge is necessary. To attain self-acceptance one has to acquire the true knowledge. The chapter 4, and Shloka 38 it is stated that knowledge is the most purifying thing in the world. One has to attain the purity of mind through prolonged practice of Yoga and self-discipline. By attaining knowledge through self-study, Yoga, and Dharma one can attain knowledge. One needs to be humble. A knowledgeable and self-realized person sees oneself in everyone and presence of everywhere. This verse emphasizes the importance of self-awareness and knowledge as a means of understanding the true nature of the self and the interconnectedness of all things. Self-acceptance is a crucial aspect of mental health and well-being of the individual. When an individual accept their reality, strengths, weaknesses they are better equipped to navigate the challenges of life and maintain positive relationships with others. The Bhagavad Gita offers insights for fostering self-awareness and personal growth. One of the primary benefits of sel-acceptance is improved mental health and the research shows that individuals who accept themselves for who they are, have lower levels of anxiety and depression and more likely to experience positive emotions (Shapira & Mongrain, 2010). This is in alignment with the teachings of the Bhagavad Gita, which emphasizes the importance of cultivating inner peace and equanimity in the face of the life's challenges.

Surrendering the fruits of one's actions is a way of letting go of attachment to external outcomes and focusing on one's inner state of being. Cultivating detachment is the first step in the direction of self-acceptance. By cultivating detachment from external outcomes, individuals can maintain a sense of inner peace and equanimity. In the face of challenges and setbacks maintaining equipoise. Mindfulness research by Keng et al. (2011) shows that individuals who are able to practice detachment are able to control their thoughts and emotions are better able to cope with stress and maintain emotional balance.

In addition to improving mental health, self-acceptance also plays a key role in fostering greater self-awareness and personal growth. Accepting themselves for who they are and identifying areas of improvement in their weaknesses, individuals can prepare with better realistic plans and take steps to improve themselves. This is consistent with the teachings of the Bhagavad Gita, which underscores the crucial role of self-reflection and self-improvement in the process of development of an individual.

Chapter 6 in Shloka 5 of the Gita states that a person can lift himself to higher consciousness by himself alone because self is the friend of oneself and the greatest enemy also. A self in higher consciousness is the best friend and a degraded self is the best enemy of a person. By accepting oneself for who one is, individuals are better equipped to face the reality of human life. The complexities of human life present a unique combination of challenges and individuals are better able to identify their strengths and weaknesses can take steps to improve themselves. Finally self-acceptance also plays an important role in relationship with others. Based on a realistic self-perception, individuals are better able to connect with other members of society at a deeper level of connection with more authenticity in relationships. This is because self-acceptance allows individuals to be more open and vulnerable which in turn focuses on fostering greater trust, accountability, originality, transparency, and stability in relationships. Cultivation of inner peace and detachment makes individuals better in the manner of capacity to connect with others from a place of authenticity and openness.

The Bhagavad Gita emphasizes the importance of social relationships and guides the way to cultivation of healthy social and personal relationships with others. Chapter 2, Shloka 47 teaches individuals practical guidance for remaining equipoised by abandonment of attachment to success or failure. This evenness of mind – the control of desires is result of disciplined character and Yoga. This verse underscores the importance of maintaining equanimity and detachment in all aspects of life and practicing the connection with the supreme soul. By cultivation of inner peace and detachment, individuals are better equipped to relate with others from a place of authenticity, humanity and openness.

Studies have shown empirical evidence of the relationship between self-acceptance and others. Individuals who have a realistic view of self, tends to be more constructive towards their criticism which opens new avenues for social dialogue and enhanced understanding (Wagner & Cartwright, 2021). It leads to positive interactions with others and creates a sense of authenticity and honesty in relationships with others. In the case of an acceptance of the true self, individuals understand the uniqueness of every perspective and learn to accept and appreciate the views and qualities of others, leading to more harmonious and fulfilling relationships (Wagner & Cartwright, 2021).

In addition to improved social relationships, self-acceptance can also foster a positive impact on intimate relationships between two individuals. Research has demonstrated that high level of self-acceptance is associated with greater emotional intimacy and higher level of satisfaction in relationships with their partners (Berman & Davis, 2018). By making individuals feel more comfortable and content with their imperfections and limitations, self-acceptance provides greater emotional intimacy and a deeper connection with their partners.

Thus, overall, self-acceptance plays a crucial role in the promotion of mental health and well-being for fostering greater self-awareness and personal growth of individuals and it improves relationships with others also. By accepting ourselves, we can live a more authentic, satisfying and healthy social and personal life which is more fulfilling and free from the constraints of societal expectations and our own internalized beliefs.

Obstacles to Self-Acceptance

Despite the numerous benefits of self-acceptance, individuals may struggle to fully harness the benefits of it. The main cause is that people don't accept themselves as they are. There are several common barriers to self-acceptance which include several societal and external norms and internalized beliefs of individuals.

One major obstacle to self-acceptance is the societal pressure which reinforce individuals to conform to social pressure. The internalized norms and values are also a major source of conflict internally for individuals. These internalized beliefs naturally create expectations which can lead individuals to feel inadequate and unworthy, which leads to search for an idealized version of themselves that may not be attainable or authentic. This can lead to negative and distorted self-talk and feelings of shame making it difficult to fully accept themselves (Nelf, 2011).

Internalized beliefs and self-judgement may present some of the significant barriers to self-acceptance leading to individuals holding negative self-beliefs that have been ingrained in them from childhood. Some parents already enforce negative self-beliefs in children such as, "You are not good in some specific academic discipline or social interaction, I am not good in this or that." These beliefs can be deeply rooted in the unconscious of the individual and may lead to feelings of unworthiness and self-doubt. Apart from this, it can create a false sense of identity that may intervene negatively in adjusting with the social interactions and unique demands due to varied external factors in society such as wealth, status and achievement.

However there are several strategies suggested by scholars to overcome these barriers to foster better self-acceptance. The Gita emphasizes the importance of understanding the true nature of self, submission to the higher power and detaching oneself from the outcomes of the action and false ego. This detachment and surrender to higher spiritual self allows individuals to recognize their true selves, and to recognize that self is not tied to external factors but is a part of the divine indestructible and immortal supreme power that exists within all beings.

The Gita also teaches the importance of mindfulness and self-awareness for overcoming internalized beliefs and negative self-concept and self-talk. It is said in Gita that by becoming more aware of one's cognitive processes, emotions, and actions; one can begin to challenge negative self-beliefs and replace them with more positive and self-compassionate ones. The Gita emphasizes the practice of self-inquiry to ask questions related to existence of a person such as "who I am" and what is "my true nature"? The practice of self-inquiry helps individuals to understand them that they are the part of universal consciousness.

Additionally, the Gita underscores the importance of self-compassion and non-judgement in the journey towards a broader self-acceptance conforming to the reality of the society and universe. This can help in practicing individuals letting go of the self-judgement and negative self-talk and self-perceptions and embrace their true selves. In conclusion, despite several obstacles to self-acceptance individuals can master self-acceptance by practicing surrender to higher spiritual self which is abiding to all conscious and unconscious beings, detachment, mindfulness, self-inquiry and self-compassion. The teachings of the Gita provide valuable guidance on how to cultivate self-acceptance and remain happy and improve the well-being and live a more authentic and fulfilling life.

Chapter 18
Interconnectedness in Gita

Interconnectedness refers to the idea that everything in this cosmos is interconnected, interdependent and complementary. This simply means that all living beings, the creation of humans—culture, civilization and man-made architectures influence human lives and are interconnected with each other in various ways. The interconnectedness needs an analysis from the perspective of systems thinking where complex systems are examined by understanding the interconnection of parts and relationships. This concept has been explored across various disciplinary fields of philosophy, sociology, ecology, management and systems theory. Basically, if we examine a system from a perspective of wholeness and connectedness, we can understand the interconnectedness of the parts and whole, the processes and their alignment with the systemic goals.

In practice, interconnectedness can be seen in many ways in social life and academic research. Interconnectedness of environmental systems could be examined using the principle that any change in any part of the system would affect the functioning of entire system. Similarly social systems are complex and are composed of connected parts of social institutions, norms, values, and individual actors are also integrated in it. Any change or influence in any part of social system may affect other parts in various ways by different mechanisms.

Recognizing the interconnectedness of things in systems such as social, economic, political, and cultural contexts can help us understand complex problems and identify potential solutions. This way a sustainable and equitable future could be restored for entire humanity.

Psychological perspective of Interconnectedness

From a psychological perspective, interconnectedness can be seen as an important element of human life which is instrumental in achieving well-being, resilience, personal development, social life and belongingness. Attachment theory advocates this position that humans are inherently and biologically wired to form close and emotional bonds with others.

According to the attachment theory, the quality of these emotional bonds can have a significant impact on an individual's psychological development, moral development, social development and overall personality development. Secure attachment bonds foster belief in the social life, restoring belief in social and political systems. What could be expected from a socially and emotionally deprived person who doesn't have any source of emotional dependency and is incomplete? Secure attachment bonds foster trust, empathy and mutual support and help in producing positive outcomes in individuals. Higher self-esteem, better coping strategies and greater resilience in the face of adversity could be fostered with enhancing the interconnectedness in individuals.

Conversely, when people are tied with insecure, unreliable bonds and there is lack of trust, emotional distance and poor communication; people can have a range of negative outcomes, such as depression, anxiety and poor interpersonal relationships. This could lead to an unfulfilled and frustrated life which would be counterproductive and detrimental for the social fabric and health of society.

Beyond attachment theory, there are various other psychological perspectives such as social identity theory and self-determination theory, which emphasizes the crucial role of interpersonal connections and a sense of belonging to others for psychological well-being and a fulfilled life. These theories advocate that the feeling of connection to others can help individuals develop a sense of purpose, meaning and autonomy in their lives.

The psychological perspective of interconnectedness emphasizes the importance of Gita's ancient wisdom in developing healthy social relationships which are necessary for carrying social responsibilities of a person. Avoidance of responsibilities is the only way to escape the social connectivity in the framework provided by Gita. This is not possible and permissible for even an enlightened and most powerful person in society. Krishna mentions at one place that despite not having any obligation to involve in the matter of this world, he reincarnates himself and performs his duties. This concept of Lokasamgraha in Gita is based on its emphasis on Karma. Recognizing the interconnectedness as pivotal to performance of social duties is necessary for promoting social bonds, mental health and resilience.

The psychological perspective of interconnectedness emphasizes its importance in social life and human relationships for individual well-being and development of society. Recognizing that interconnectedness is vital for fostering well-being in individuals is crucial.

Karma in Srimad Bhagavad Gita is the concept of cause and effect suggesting that every action has consequences rippling through time and space. The concept of Vedic Rita, the universal law of society and nature is given a new definition in Gita. In fact, it is replaced by the principle of Karma. The principle of Karma is basically emphasizing the centrality of human agency within the broader perspective of societal norms. Without social norms and values, understanding and interpreting agency is a difficult and meaningless effort. Mere emphasis on individual goals, insatiable desires and unguided action without consideration of social factors may result in certain kind of chaos. In Chapter 2, Shloka 47, Krishna says that prescribed duty is the only way to achieve peace and tranquility. He further emphasizes detachment from the fruits of action and says to never consider yourself to be the cause of the results of your activities, and never be attached to not doing your duty. This verse highlights that human actions are interconnected and can't be seen as isolated events. As a part of larger wave of social structure and institutions laid by Dharma and Karma, the actions of human beings are part of a larger system which is bounded by interdependent chain of cause and effect (Action and result). One more thing is clear that when we align our actions with the framework of Dharma, and don't expect the results or worry about them, we universally connect ourselves with the global consciousness and collective consciousness. Thus, interconnectedness becomes larger part of our evolution towards a global consciousness.

Dharma as a central concept in the Gita emphasizes the path or righteousness and duty. Dharma is closely related to karma which suggests that our actions should be guided by the perspective of Dharma. Dharma works as an overarching framework for guiding actions in normal course of life as well as in specific or in situations of crisis. Krishna explains the importance of Dharma to Arjuna in Chapter 3, verse 35 that performance of one's own duties is better than mastering the duties of other persons. By fulfilling the righteous paths and responsibilities assigned by Dharma a person never comes to grief. This verse also connects individuals within the broader framework of Dharma by assigned duties, responsibilities, and social relationships. The cosmic interconnectedness in Gita suggests that each individual has a unique and prescribed role in the cosmic order of relationships of beings. Thus, by simply fulfilling our duties and responsibilities, an individual can contribute to the larger well-being and good of the spiritual evolution of society and self.

Gita emphasizes the importance of Yoga as a path of spiritual practice for controlling senses, understanding self, promoting self-reflection giving strength to follow the path of righteousness or Dharma. Yoga gives capacity of self-discipline, control, perseverance, and enables a person for pursuing spiritual practice and self-realization. It is closely related with Karma and Dharma indicating that an individual's spiritual evolution is intimately connected to his actions and sense of duty in the world. Krishna explains the importance of yoga to Arjuna in Chapter 6, Shloka 46 by emphasizing that following one's prescribed duties is the only way to attain perfection in this world. The path of Karma Yoga also leads to self-realization. This verse highlights the relatedness of all beings by suggesting that the path of yoga is not just a solitary practice of meditation in caves or close rooms or on stages, but it is intimately connected to the broader concept of Dharma which is necessary for operating society. Through the practice of Karma yoga, one connects his actions to the broader social goals, develops a sense of detachment from results that is the best way to refrain from desires and stay away from resulting frustration if the goals are not fulfilled. Interesting thing is that Gita doesn't promote purposelessness by saying that one should not expect the result, but the goals are set by Dharma and prescribed Karma. So purpose is fulfilling one's Dharma by dutifulness. The duties of individuals are not self-centered, they are designed in Dharma in a way that becomes pivotal for the smooth functioning of society.

The Gita also emphasizes the interconnectedness of all beings through its teachings on non-dualism (Advaita). It suggests that all beings, living and non-living are originated from the God, and when the cosmic manifestation is dissolved (The State of Pralay in Hindu Mythology), they merge into the unmanifest again (Chapter 7, verse 19). This verse highlights the interconnectedness of all beings and their common origin and connection to god. At one place Lord Krishna says that one who sees everyone as me, and me in everyone is not hidden from me and I am not hidden from him. This Advaita or unity of individuals in human society promotes a sense of worth of every individual and a deeper awareness of our interconnectedness with all beings. The identities, ego, and differences are illusory and only apparent at practical aspect of human behavior and we all are part of the larger cosmic order that transcends time and space.

The message of Gita about cosmic interconnectedness has important implications for how we live our lives and interact with others suggests that our actions and decisions are not just isolated to ourselves but they create a larger web of cause and effect affecting the world around us. So, Dharma provides a frame of reference for connecting individuals with responsibilities and duties which are needed for creating a positive impact on society. The interconnectedness is also emphasized by postmodern thinkers like Lyotard.

Finally, the message of interconnectedness in the Gita highlights the importance of cultivating a sense of detachment from the results of our actions and a deeper awareness of our interconnectedness with the cosmic order and social life. Once, a person understands the interconnectedness of all human beings he knows that harming anyone is a kind of self-harm. It has implications for environmental ethics in the sense that Gita recognizes living and non-living beings as a singular unity as an intrinsic quality of Krishna, the God. Thus plants, mountains, animals are all indistinguishable from God. At one place Krishna says (Chapter 10, Verse 26) I am the fig tree among trees. When Krishna identifies himself with tree, it has vast implications for the Hindu culture in the area of environmental ethics. It reflects the alignment of the Gita with modern environmental ethics which advocates for accepting trees, greenery, forests as important part of human life and sustainability. By identifying this oneness with nature and other human beings, Gita promotes a sense of compassion and empathy for other humans and environment for a more just and equitable world.

It can be said that overall, the message of interconnectedness in the Bhagavad Gita is a powerful reminder of the unity of all things and importance of living our lives with a sense of purpose derived from Dharma which advocates for associated living and coherence with nature in unity. It offers a path of spiritual practice and self-realization that is intimately connected to our actions and sense of duty in the world that has potential to transform the lives of humans and contemporary society around us.

In conclusion, the message of interconnectedness in the Bhagavad Gita is a powerful reminder of our interconnectedness with all beings and the larger cosmic order which includes living and non-living beings, nature and humans. It gives equal weight to all human beings and other flora and fauna. It has a message for contemporary movement of sustainability which emphasizes living in accordance with nature. Its teachings on Karma, Dharma, Yoga and detachment are guiding principles for understanding the unity of all human beings and nature. The emphasis on dutifulness is not self-centered but a social responsibility. Krishna himself says at one place that he reincarnates himself for promoting the daily business and order of social life. The famous Shloka— Yada Yada Hi Dharmasya Glanir Bhavati Bharata (Chapter 4, Shloka 7 and 8) reflects the commitment of Shri Krishna towards the society to maintain the law and order. Moreover, the concept of Lokasamgraha is also similar to this where he highlights that despite not having any obligation to maintain this world, he reincarnates and indulges himself in the daily business of the world as a common man. Though it's called a play or Leela for him, and doesn't accumulate Karma because Krishna presents the ideal of Karma and Dharma. This has important implications for our lives, social interactions and approach towards environmental sustainability and social justice.

CHAPTER 19
Self-reflection in Gita

Chapter 3 (Shloka 40) emphasizes the importance of self-reflection. Self-reflection has implications for regulating the senses, disciplining the mind, strengthening the intellect and redirecting desires towards just causes. Senses are primary interface with outer world. Mind consolidates the data and magnifies attachment into strong desires. The intellect provides judgment but can be swayed away by strong emotions or desires. Only the knowledge of true self can help in navigating life meaningfully.

It can be said that Srimad Bhagavad Gita includes several psychological concepts of educational implications such as Emotional Intelligence, Mindfulness, Self-awareness, Self-regulation, Resilience, Perseverance, Compassion, Authenticity, Transcendence, Self-transformation, Ego transcendence, Mind-body connection, Self-compassion, Forgiveness, Self-acceptance, Non-judgmental awareness, Interconnectedness, Graciousness, Mind-body integration, Self-transcendence, Freedom from attachment and Self-reflection. It offers valuable insights whether read as a spiritual text, a philosophical treatise, or a guide.

The Gita advocates the universality of the Self and self-reflection as a key element of self-awareness. Self is undivided

Table 19: Concept of Self -reflection in Srimad Bhagavad Gita

Aspect	Concept of Self in Gita	Insights from Modern Perspectives	Key Representative Citations
Universality of Self	The self is undivided and universal, reflecting oneness across all beings (Gita 6.29).	Self is often seen as individual and unique to each person, though some philosophies explore collective consciousness.	Sneed & Whitbourne (2003); D'Argembeau et al. (2008); Elder et al. (2023)
Immortality of Self	Self is eternal, unborn, and ever-existing (Gita Chapter 2). It transcends life and death. **(Gita Chapter 2, Shloka 20)**	Self is often tied to psychological constructs and identity, typically viewed as temporal and influenced by life events.	Sneed & Whitbourne (2003); Wu et al. (2010)
Self as the Real Subject	Self is the ultimate subject of knowledge, understood through inner reflection and yoga (Gita 6.15). **(Gita Chapter 6, Shloka 15)**	Reflection leads to deeper understanding of one's inner self and facilitates mature identity formation.	Holt et al. (2010); Faith et al. (2024)

Aspect	**Concept of Self in Gita**	**Insights from Modern Perspectives**	**Key Representative Citations**
Role of Discipline	Controlling and disciplining the self through yoga brings peace and stability (Gita 6.6). **(Gita Chapter 6, Shloka 6)**	Self-regulation techniques such as mindfulness and emotional intelligence aid in developing discipline.	Takano & Tanno (2009); Tiuraniemi et al. (2010)
Inner Reflection	Focused contemplation helps understand the self beyond outer distractions (Gita 6.15). **(Gita Chapter 6, Shloka 15)**	Introspection, therapy, and structured self-awareness exercises are modern methods for self-understanding.	Spendelow & Butler (2015); Sim et al. (2020)
Self as Immutable	Self is stable, immutable, and connected to the Supreme Self (Gita Chapter 6, Shloka 7).	The self is dynamic and continually evolves through experiences, though spiritual traditions often highlight a stable essence.	Wu et al. (2010); Bird & Caligor (2024)

Aspect	Concept of Self in Gita	Insights from Modern Perspectives	Key Representative Citations
Supreme Self	The Supreme Self (Krishna) resides in the hearts of all beings (Gita Chapter 18, Shloka 61).	Reflection on spirituality as a core aspect of identity adds depth to understanding the self.	Wu et al. (2010); Doris (2016)
Self-Contentment	Achieving self-contentment involves giving up desires and limiting attachments (Gita Chapter 2, Shloka 55).	Contentment is often linked to managing expectations, achieving goals, and balancing personal desires with reality.	Sneed & Whitbourne (2003); Takano & Tanno (2009)
Action and Inaction	Self remains unchanging amidst action and inaction; duty-bound actions without attachment liberate from Karma (Gita Chapter 4, Shloka 18).	Ethical frameworks often emphasize intention and social impact rather than spiritual detachment.	Kao et al. (2017); Akhurst (2020)

Aspect	Concept of Self in Gita	Insights from Modern Perspectives	Key Representative Citations
Moral Responsibility	Inaction in the face of evil is itself a sin; fulfilling one's duty aligns with Dharma and leads to liberation.	Reflection aids in evaluating ethical responsibilities and aligning actions with societal and personal values.	Adams et al. (2022); Henderson et al. (2023)
Crisis Management	A disciplined self stays calm during crises and maintains equanimity in honor or dishonor (Gita 6.6). **(Gita Chapter 6, Shloka 6)**	Reflection enhances resilience, emotional regulation, and adaptive coping mechanisms in adversity.	Takano & Tanno (2009); Faith et al. (2024)
Definition of Self-Regulation	Realization of the Self (Atman) as eternal consciousness and aligning actions with self-knowledge for self-mastery. (Gita 2.55; 5.24).	Combines psychological focus on behavioral control with the Gita's spiritual emphasis on self-realization and purpose.	Prasko et al. (2012); Martin & McLellan (2007)

Aspect	**Concept of Self in Gita**	**Insights from Modern Perspectives**	**Key Representative Citations**
Goal Setting	Swadharma (one's duty) and Nishkama Karma (selfless action) emphasize meaningful, ethical goals (Gita Chapter 3, Shloka 35).	Goal-setting is central to self-regulation and achieving life purpose.	Tiuraniemi et al. (2010); Newman et al. (2022)
Emotional Regulation	Sthitaprajna (steady wisdom) emphasizes emotional stability through detachment from outcomes (Gita Chapter 2, Shlokas 55-57).	Emotional regulation strategies, including mindfulness and reflection, are critical for managing stress and negative emotions.	Kao et al. (2017); Bird & Caligor (2024)
Behavioral Regulation	Karma Yoga stresses disciplined action and purification of the mind through selfless deeds (Gita Chapter 3, Shlokas 8, 19).	Aligns disciplined behavior with selfless service for holistic self-regulation.	Adams et al. (2022); Sim et al. (2020)

Aspect	Concept of Self in Gita	Insights from Modern Perspectives	Key Representative Citations
Mechanisms of Regulation	Practices like Shravana (listening), Manana (reflection), and Nididhyasana (meditation) enhance self-regulation (Gita Chapter 6, Shloka 15).	Structured reflective practices enhance personal growth and self-regulation.	Prasko et al. (2012); Sim et al. (2020)
Challenges	Ignorance, attachment, and dominance of Rajas and Tamas hinder self-regulation (Gita 14.5-8; 3.36-37).	Reflection helps identify and overcome obstacles like cognitive overload, conflicting goals, and emotional dysregulation.	Takano & Tanno (2009); Sinha (2023)
Social Implications	Lokasangraha (welfare of society) emphasizes self-regulation as a path to collective good and moral leadership (Gita Chapter 3, Shloka 20).	Reflection promotes societal well-being and ethical leadership.	Akhurst (2020); Ramos (2017)

Aspect	Concept of Self in Gita	Insights from Modern Perspectives	Key Representative Citations
Applications to Education	Aligning educational goals with self-awareness and character building through Swadharma (Gita Chapter 18, Shloka 45).	Reflective teaching practices improve student self-awareness and professional skills.	Newman et al. (2022); Tiuraniemi et al. (2010)

and universal which reflects oneness across all beings (Gita, Chapter 6, Shloka 29). Modern psychological perspectives see self as individual and unique to each person though some philosophies explore collective consciousness. Immortality of self is a central concept in Gita which emphasizes that self is eternal, unborn and ever-existing (Gita Chapter 2) and it transcends life and Death (Gita Chapter 2, Shloka 20). Modern psychology sees self as a psychological construct and identity, and typically views it as temporal and influenced and shaped by life events. Self as a real subject is emphasized in Gita which says that self is the ultimate subject of knowledge and understanding it through inner reflection and yoga (Gita Chapter 6, Shloka 15). Modern psychologists found that reflection leads to deeper understanding of one's inner self and facilitates mature identity formation (Holt et al., 2010; Faith et al., 2024). Role of discipline is emphasized in Gita. Controlling and disciplining the self through Yoga brings peace and stability (Gita Chapter 6, Shloka 6). Modern psychological perspective emphasize self-regulation techniques such as mindfulness and emotional intelligence in developing discipline (Tokano & Tanno, 2009; Tiruaneimi et al., 2010). Gita promotes inner reflection focused contemplation which helps understand the self beyond outer distractions (Gita Chapter 6, Shloka 15). Modern psychology finds that introspection, therapy and structured self-awareness exercises are modern methods for self-understanding (Spendelow & Butler, 2015; Sim et al., 2020). Self as immutable and stable object is highlighted in Gita (Chapter 6, Shloka 7). In modern psychology self is dynamic and continually evolving through experiences. Supreme self is the ultimate self in Gita which contains all selves and is the ultimate source of creation of the living and non-living beings. (Gita Chapter 18, Shloka 61). Modern psychology finds that reflection on spirituality is a core aspect of identity which adds depth to the understanding of the self (Wu et al., 2010; Doris, 2016). Gita emphasizes self-contentment as a measure to control the senses and expectation of results for promoting detachment and Nishkama Karma (Gita Chapter 2, Shloka 55). Contentment is often linked to managing expectations, achieving goals and balancing personal desires with reality which leads to self-realization (Sneed & Whitbourne, 2003; Takano & Tanno, 2009). Action and inaction are central themes in Gita which emphasizes that self remains unchanging amidst action and inaction; and duty bound actions without attachment liberate from Karma (Gita Chapter 4, Shloka 18). Modern psychological and ethical frameworks often emphasize intention and social impact over spiritual detachment and detached action (Kao et al., 2017; Akhurst, 2020).

Gita strongly proposes that inaction in the face of evil is itself a sin and fulfilling one's duty aligns with Dharma and leads to liberation. Although modern perspectives find that reflection aids in evaluating ethical responsibilities and aligning actions with societal and personal values (Adams et al., 2022; Henderson et al., 2023). In the crisis management self-reflection is an important part and Gita highlights that disciplined self stays calm during crises and maintains equanimity in honor or dishonor (Gita Chapter 6, Shloka 6). The importance of reflection in self-regulation is also highlighted as realizing self as eternal consciousness and aligning actions with self-knowledge for self-mastery (Gita Chapter 2, Shloka 55; Gita Chapter 5, Shloka 24). Staying in Swadharma (One's duty) and Nishkama Karma (Selfless action) are necessary for living a purposeful life and goal setting according to Gita. Modern psychology approves the notion that goal-setting is central to self-regulation and achieving life purpose (Tiuraniemi et al., 2010; Newman et al.,2022). Emotional regulation is emphasized in

Gita as Sthitaprajna (Steady Wisdom) for achieving emotional stability through detachment from outcomes (Gita Chapter 2, Shlokas 55-57). Emotional regulation strategies, including mindfulness and reflection are critical for managing stress and negative emotional outcomes (Kao et al., 2017; Newman et al., 2022)

One possible model of self-reflection based on the Gita could be structured around the following steps:

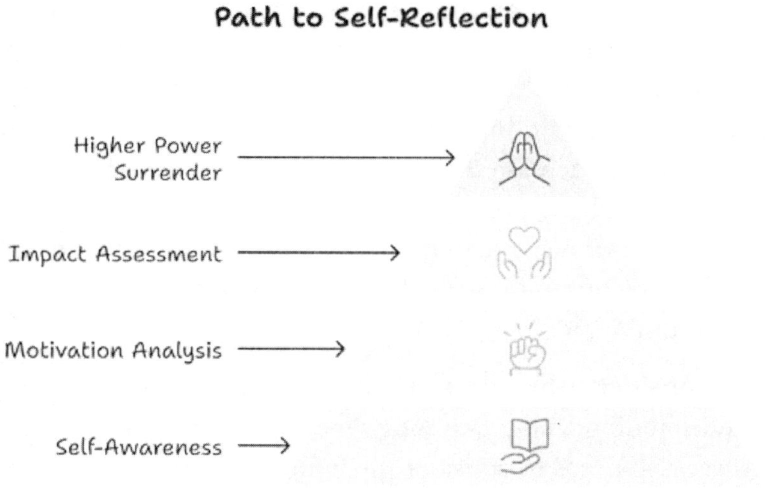

Figure 6: Path to Self-reflection in Gita

Cultivate self-awareness: this is the first step in self-reflection and its aim is to develop an awareness of one's thoughts, feelings, and actions in individual by understanding the true nature of self as emphasized in Gita which is immortal, perennial, and connected to supreme self. This can be attained by meditation, yoga or journaling which allow individuals to observe their inner experiences and keep a track of their own spiritual progress. Several Gita-inspired mindfulness based therapies have demonstrated the power to improve the state of self-awareness.

This can be done through practices such as meditation, yoga, or journaling, which allow individuals to observe their inner experience without judgment.

Examine one's motivations: Once self-awareness has been established, one needs to understand the pattern of his desires and willingness to work as a detached person. If one starts working selflessly and detached as per the prescribed Dharma or the Standard Operating Procedure, he could be more aware about his actions and motivations. These motivations could be in the form of one's thoughts, feelings and actions. Questioning oneself during the course of action and decision such as: what am I seeking to achieve? What is driving me Dharma or some distractions? Am I controlled by my intellect or being driven by only senses and their subjects? Am I acting out of pressure, fear, desire or a sense of detached selfless duty?

Consider the impact on others: In addition to understanding and examining one's own motivations and drives, one needs to consider the impact of actions on others and broader society. Gita is never focused on narrow self-interests, but it is based on the concept of Loksamgraha (The public good). So considering the impact on others is a central point of self-reflection. This involves development of a sense of empathy and broader interconnectedness with society and nature. Asking questions such as : How this decision may impact our society and connected ones? Is my working style respectful and compassionate towards others? These types of questions which are concerned with understanding the impact of one's actions on broader social good are necessary to have clear self-reflection.

Surrender to a higher power: The final step in the

model of self-reflection is to surrender to a higher power—The Supreme self. This includes that the individual understands the limitations of his own drives, self and cultivates a faith in some higher spiritual order, develops a sense of humility and openness to the unknown and chaotic nature of results of the Karmas in practical life. This acceptance will help him in getting rid of the frustrations from undesired outcomes and contingencies in life.

This model of self-reflection could be integrated into the curriculum and pedagogy in various ways. Educators can incorporate practices of mindfulness meditation or reflective writing on how the students are aware of their own selves, an analysis of their academic drives and broader motivations about life and achievements. Students could be promoted to understand the impact of their any decision on his life, family life and the broader social life. Finally cultivating a habit to surrendering outcomes to the higher spiritual self would enable them to take a position of equanimity in their lives and would help them remain balanced during the situation of crisis.

In daily life, the model of self-reflection based on the Srimad Bhagavad Gita can be applied in a variety of contexts including personal relationships, work, leadership and decision-making. A self-aware individual with understanding of his own motivations and a sense of interconnectedness and empathy with a knowledge of the impact of his actions on himself and others can take more wise and practical decisions as per the prescribed duties. Surrendering to higher spiritual power without any fear from authorities or pressure groups can enable individuals and decision makers in taking decisions which may foster broader individual and social good, even in the face of uncertainty and adversity. The model of self-reflection based on Gita's teachings offers valuable insights for individuals seeking personal growth and spiritual development in life. The model emphasizes cultivating a habit of self-awareness and mindfulness. Furthermore, it advocates for understanding the motives driving our behavior. Further by understanding the impact of our decisions on broader society helps us in taking right decisions as per Dharma or prescribed duties. Finally surrendering the results to supreme helps in remaining peaceful and equanimous in crisis. Thus by following the model or guidelines of the Gita can help in developing deeper connections with themselves and others and make more ethical and compassionate choices in both education and daily social life.

Chapter 20

Development of Life Satisfaction Scale

Introduction

Extensively studied as a multi-dimensional construct, life satisfaction is a broad concept in the field of psychology, industrial psychology and organizational behavior. The basic assumption of the measurement of life satisfaction construct aims to measure the degree of positive feeling which individuals feel about their lives as a whole. It includes their emotional state, social relationships, achievements and overall sense of purpose and life (Diener et al., 2018). The study of life satisfaction is particularly important as it is closely linked with a range of psychological, physical and socially desirable outcomes such as mental health, physical health, social integration and academic work performance (Diener et al., 2018; Helliwell et al., 2013). This brief synopsis as an overview of the concept of life satisfaction is based on the latest contemporary research about this concept, its conceptualization, measurement and correlates.

Life satisfaction is a complex and multifaceted construct that has been conceptualized in different ways by different researchers. Health, both physical and mental, profoundly influences satisfaction, as good health is consistently linked to higher scores (Diener & Chan, 2011; Wiest et al., 2011). Individuals adapt partially to major life events, as seen in longitudinal studies, but not all adaptations fully restore previous satisfaction levels (Lucas, 2007; Yap et al., 2011b). Cultural factors also play a significant role, with collectivist cultures emphasizing social harmony and individualist cultures prioritizing self-esteem (Suh et al., 1998; Diener & Diener, 1995).

Environmental conditions such as air quality contribute meaningfully to satisfaction, with reduced pollution associated with better outcomes (Luechinger, 2009). Life satisfaction measures are increasingly relevant in policy contexts, as seen in the UK and OECD initiatives that integrate well-being assessments into decision-making processes (Inglehart & Welzel, 2010). Finally, affective and cognitive factors, including emotions and evaluations, significantly shape satisfaction judgments, with both domains contributing to overall well-being (Diener et al., 1998; Schwarz & Strack, 1999).

Life satisfaction measures exhibit strong **reliability**, with short-term stability coefficients often exceed 0.8 and consistent correlations across instruments (Diener et al., 1985; Pavot & Diener, 1993b). **Heritability** studies suggest that genetic factors contribute 30%-50% to life satisfaction variability (Lykken & Tellegen, 1996; Stubbe et al., 2005). Economic conditions, particularly income levels and GDP, significantly correlate with satisfaction ($r = 0.83$), underscoring the impact of financial stability (Diener et al., 2010; Helliwell, 2007). Similarly, **social capital** and community relationships are vital, with greater social connectivity enhancing well-being (Helliwell, 2008; Veenhoven, 2005).

As a subjective assessment of one's overall quality of life the concept represents contentment or acceptance of life circumstances. It is distinguished from related constructs such as subjective well-being (which includes emotional components). Subjective well-being includes both cognitive (life satisfaction) and affective (positive/negative emotions) components and is a broader concept including life satisfaction. There are also Life-Domain satisfaction which focuses on specific areas like work or marriage, whereas life satisfaction is broader and general in nature.

The measurement of Life Satisfaction is measured using reliable and rigorously developed scales. Satisfaction with life scale is such a 5-item scale widely validated for measuring life satisfaction. Due to social desirability bias, cultural and gender neutrality sometimes reliability issues are raised in its measurement.

Determinants of Life satisfaction in general include debates of personality vs. Environment. Personality traits like resilience, extraversion and internal locus of control strongly correlate with stable levels of life satisfaction are found to be strongly correlated with stable levels of life satisfaction. Life events (e.g. marriage, employment changes) have short-term effects but may not sustain long-term satisfaction. So empirical research exhibits that life satisfaction is more decided by internal personality factors (Magnus et al., 1993; Suh et al., 1996).

Adaptation plays an important role in life satisfaction which is the balance between reality and expectations. Multiple-Discrepancy Theory explains satisfaction through comparisons (Michalos, 1986). Cultural influences are also important in deciding how one perceives life satisfaction. Collectivist cultures rely on norms, while individualist cultures focus on emotions. It implies that there is a connection between emotional patterns and cultural patterns. Wealthy egalitarian societies report higher satisfaction (Suh et al., 1998).

Gender doesn't differently associate with life satisfaction. Women experience more intense emotions but report similar life satisfaction as men. Women rely more on social resources and men focus on financial and occupational success. Perhaps this is the reason that men are more independent to pursue their occupations in contemporary society (Diener & Fujita, 1995; Pinquart & Sorensen, 2000). Life satisfaction remains stable or increases with age, possibily due to accommodative coping and achieving life goals (Ryff, 1991; Brandtstaedter & Renner, 1990)

Life satisfaction measures exhibit strong **reliability**, with short-term stability coefficients often exceeding 0.8 and consistent correlations across instruments (Diener et al., 1985; Pavot & Diener, 1993b). **Heritability** studies suggest that genetic factors contribute 30%-50% to life satisfaction variability (Lykken & Tellegen, 1996; Stubbe et al., 2005). Economic conditions, particularly income levels and GDP, significantly correlate with satisfaction ($r = 0.83$), underscoring the impact of financial stability (Diener et al., 2010; Helliwell, 2007). Similarly, **social capital** and community relationships are vital, with greater social connectivity enhancing well-being (Helliwell, 2008; Veenhoven, 2005).

Physical and mental health are consistently linked to higher life satisfaction scores (Diener & Chan, 2011; Wiest et al., 2011). Individuals adapt partially to major life events, as seen in longitudinal studies, but not all adaptations fully restore previous satisfaction levels (Lucas, 2007; Yap et al., 2011b). Cultural factors also play a significant role. The collectivist cultures emphasize social harmony and individualist cultures prioritize self-esteem (Suh et al., 1998; Diener & Diener, 1995).

Environmental conditions such as air quality also meaningfully contribute to satisfaction, with reduced pollution associated with better outcomes (Luechinger, 2009). Life satisfaction measures are increasingly gaining relevance in policy contexts. UK and OECD policy initiatives have integrated well-being assessments into decision-making processes (Inglehart & Welzel, 2010). Finally, affective and cognitive factors, which include emotions and evaluations can significantly influence satisfaction judgments because both domains contribute to overall well-being (Diener et al., 1998; Schwarz & Strack, 1999).

As a multifaceted and complex construct, life satisfaction has been conceptualized in various ways. Diathesis-Stress model (Lazarus, 1966) emphasizes that individual's cognitive evaluations of life events and their coping resources are more important for perceiving a higher level of satisfaction in life. Self-Determination Theory (Ryan and Deci, 2000) suggests that it is determined by the degree of autonomy, competence and relatedness. A satisfied person in life would be free to choose his path of life with competence in that domain supported by other humans as friends, family or colleagues. Relatedness is also important. So autonomy, relatedness and mastery in navigating a chosen path are important in self-determination theory.

Measurement of Life Satisfaction

Satisfaction with Life Scale (SWLS) is a multi-item scale that measures global cognitive judgements of life

Evaluating Life Satisfaction Measures

Satisfaction with Life Scale (SWLS) offers cognitive evaluation of life as a whole and its primary use involves research, individual-level studies with a high reliability of alpha value of 0.80-.95. The instrument focuses on global judgments and does not include affect or domains.

Cantril's Ladder of Life Scale measures overall life evaluation based on best and worst life scenarios and is used for global assessment of life satisfaction. The tool is highly reliable with Cronbach's alpha higher than 0.80.

Diener, Oishi, & Tay (2012) developed domain specific life satisfaction scale, with dimensions that vary according to the domain of life. Satisfaction in specific domains (e.g., health, income, family) is measured by this instrument and it is focused on research and policy evaluation. The major drawback of this instrument is that it cannot provide a holistic view of life satisfaction. Longitudinal panel studies have been conducted on multiple dimensions and areas of life, which measure changes in satisfaction over time, stability vs. adaptation and long-term well-being trends with high time series consistency. This method is expensive and requires long-term commitment (Lucas, Clark, Georgellis, & Diener.,2003, 2004; Fujita & Diener.,2005).

Conclusion

Life satisfaction is a complex and multidimensional construct and due to its focus on measuring overall satisfaction with life measured in the field of psychology, management and organizational contexts, it has gained prominence in these days. Although there is no consensus on the exact components that contribute to the life satisfaction. Research has identified

Table 20: A Review of Available Life Satisfaction Scales

Scale/Tool	Items	Dimensions Assessed	Primary Use	Reliability	Key Limitations	Citations
Satisfaction with Life Scale (SWLS)	5	Cognitive evaluation of life as a whole.	Research, individual-level studies	High (α = 0.80–0.96)	Focuses on global judgments; does not include affect or domains.	Diener, Emmons, Larsen, & Griffin (1985); Pavot & Diener (1993).
Single-Item Life Satisfaction Measures	1	Overall life satisfaction.	Large-scale surveys	Moderate (0.60–0.72)	Lower reliability; sensitive to mood/context effects.	Lucas & Donnellan (2011); World Values Survey (WVS).

Scale/Tool	Items	Dimensions Assessed	Primary Use	Reliability	Key Limitations	Citations
Cantril's Ladder of Life Scale	1 (visual)	Overall life evaluation based on best/worst life scenarios.	Global assessments	High (r = 0.80+)	Limited nuance; influenced by transient events.	Gallup World Poll; Cantril (1965).
Domain-Specific Satisfaction Scales	Varies	Satisfaction in specific domains (e.g., health, income, family).	Focused research, policy evaluation	Varies (α = 0.70+)	Cannot provide a holistic view of life satisfaction.	Diener, Oishi, & Tay (2012).

Scale/Tool	Items	Dimensions Assessed	Primary Use	Reliability	Key Limitations	Citations
Informant Reports	Varies	Perceived life satisfaction from external observers.	Validity enhancement	Moderate ($r = \sim 0.42$)	Limited knowledge of the target's subjective experience.	Sandvik, Diener, & Seidlitz (1993); Schneider & Schimmack (2009).
Longitudinal Panel Studies	Multiple (repeated)	Changes in satisfaction over time; stability vs. adaptation.	Long-term well-being trends	High (time-series consistency)	Expensive; requires long-term commitment.	Lucas, Clark, Georgellis, & Diener (2003, 2004); Fujita & Diener (2005).

Scale/Tool	Items	Dimensions Assessed	Primary Use	Reliability	Key Limitations	Citations
Psychometric and Physiological Measures	Variable	Biological/ genetic underpinnings, physiological markers.	Objective research validation	N/A (context-specific)	Limited scalability; specialized expertise required.	Lykken & Tellegen (1996); DeNeve (2011); Urry et al. (2004).

several key predictors. Social support, psychological well-being, personality and contextual factors are important forces influencing life satisfaction. These factors help us in understanding the importance of the construct of life satisfaction for theoretical and practical reasons. The implications involve developing interventions enhancing the positive perception of life in individuals, the overall well-being of society and quality of life. Future researchers can explore the complex and intricate relationships between these factors and their relative effects on life satisfaction over time.

The Concept of Life Satisfaction in the Srimad Bhagavad Gita

The concept of life satisfaction in the Srimad Bhagavad Gita could be seen in the concepts of Dharma, Artha, Kama and Moksha- The four Purusharthas. Bhakti adds into this as a main theme of the revered Hindu text as devotion towards the supreme reality. These five dimensions are interrelated and interdependent in providing a holistic view of the purposes of life and life satisfaction to lead a fulfilling and meaningful life.

Dharma, the first dimension, refers to one's duty or moral obligations. Dharma explains the universal causes which are essential for determining the individual's course of life. These are prescribed duties by shastras or scriptures for an individual in order to maintain individual peace, tranquility and social order. Dharma includes detached dutifulness and non-expectation of results. Following Dharma inculcates a sense of purpose and meaning in life which contributes to the overall life satisfaction of an individual.

The second dimension of life Artha, demonstrates the importance of material possession and financial prosperity of individual. The importance of money and material cannot be ignored in this economic world. Bhagavad Gita doesn't see money and financial possession as an end but as a means to live the dutiful life and higher spiritual goals of life. Lord Krishna advises Arjuna, the protagonist of the Gita that kingship is the mean of serving the broader duty of a king or Kshatriya. By doing so, individuals can find satisfaction in their financial security because it enables them to serve their prescribed social duties and to make a positive impact on the world.

The third dimension of Kama, which deals with sensual pleasure and desire, indicates that for a balanced life we need to control our desires and sensual pleasures with the true knowledge of our selves. This needs controlling our desires and actions with yoga and self-control. Lord Krishna teaches Arjuna to detach himself from senses in Chapter 6, Shloka 6 – One needs to control his mind as mind is the best friend or worst enemy of the individual. By practicing self-control, individuals can find a balance and satisfaction in their lives. It enhances their ability to manage their desires and achieve a sense of inner peace.

The fourth dimension of Moksha is one of the highest goals according to the Srimad Bhagavad Gita. It refers to the spiritual liberation of the people by practicing disciplined life as a spiritual person by practicing yoga, fulfilling right desires (kama) by rightly earned livelihood (Artha). By attainment of Moksha, a person becomes yogi who knows the oneness of the part and the whole (Supreme). Lord Krishna advised Arjuna to seek moksha by practicing devotion to supreme, selfless detached action, meditation and following his Dharma—his nature of Kshatriyas to fight for a just cause. By practicing Dharma, Artha and Kama; Moksha is attained which can help in finding satisfaction in the spiritual goal and pursuit of a higher purpose.

Table 21: Life Satisfaction Scale (Based on Gita)

S. No	Dimension	Items	Strongly Disagree	Disagree	Neutral	Agree	Strongly Agree
1.	Dharma	1. I feel a strong sense of purpose and meaning in my life.					
		2. I am satisfied with the way I fulfill my responsibilities and obligations.					
		3. I am living according to my values and principles.					
		4. I feel a sense of fulfillment when I help others.					
		5. I am proud of the work that I do.					

S. No	Dimension	Items	Strongly Disagree	Disagree	Neutral	Agree	Strongly Agree
		6. I feel that my life has a positive impact on others.					
2.	Artha	1. I am satisfied with my financial situation.					
		2. I am able to provide for my basic needs and the needs of my family.					
		3. I am able to save money for the future.					
		4. I am able to enjoy material pleasures without feeling guilty.					
		5. I am able to pursue my passions and interests.					

S. No	Dimension	Items	Strongly Disagree	Disagree	Neutral	Agree	Strongly Agree
		6. I am able to give back to my community and support charitable causes.					
3.	Kama	1. I am able to enjoy sensual pleasures in a balanced and healthy way.					
		2. I am able to control my desires and impulses.					
		3. I am able to find joy and pleasure in simple things.					
		4. I am able to appreciate beauty and art in the world.					
		5. I am able to connect with others in meaningful and fulfilling ways.					

S. No	Dimension	Items	Strongly Disagree	Disagree	Neutral	Agree	Strongly Agree
		6. I am able to find peace and contentment in my own company.					
4.	Moksha	1. I feel a strong sense of spiritual connection and purpose.					
		2. I am able to let go of attachments and desires.					
		3. I am able to see the interconnectedness of all things.					
		4. I am able to find inner peace and stillness.					

S. No	Dimension	Items	Strongly Disagree	Disagree	Neutral	Agree	Strongly Agree
		5. I am able to cultivate compassion and love for all beings.					
		6. I am able to accept the inevitability of change and impermanence.					
5.	Bhakti	1. I feel a deep sense of devotion and surrender to a higher power or God.					
		2. I am able to find meaning and purpose in my spiritual practices.					
		3. I am able to connect with others who share my spiritual beliefs.					

S. No	Dimension	Items	Strongly Disagree	Disagree	Neutral	Agree	Strongly Agree
		4. I am able to find guidance and wisdom in spiritual teachings.					
		5. I am able to find comfort and solace in times of difficulty through my spiritual beliefs.					
		6. I am able to find strength and resilience through my spiritual practices.					

Finally Bhakti has been identified in this study as a fifth dimension which relates to the practice of devotion towards the ultimate being or supreme power. The Bhagavad Gita teaches that devotion to God or Krishna is the key to attain the ultimate knowledge and intelligence. Bhakti needs transcendence of ego which can provide individuals with a sense of comfort, guidance and strength. Lord Krishna tells Arjuna "Leave all the Dharmas and surrender to me only, I will free you from all the sins and show the way to the righteousness (Chapter 18, Shloka 66). By cultivating devotion individuals can find satisfaction in their connection to the divine and their trust in a higher power of God.

In summary, it can be said that concept of life satisfaction in the Bhagavad Gita can be organized around four purusharthas and Bhakti. These five dimensions provide a comprehensive framework for understanding the role of purpose, meaning and fulfilment in their lives. By practicing Dharma, Artha, Kama, Moksha and Bhakti; individuals can attain self-control, fulfill their moral obligations, accumulate wealth through righteous means, pursue spiritual growth and cultivate devotion. This would help them achieve a sense of inner peace and satisfaction.

Validation of the Life Satisfaction Scale

Development of the Initial Draft: The Life Satisfaction Scale was initially developed with 40 items on the basis of identified five dimensions of Dharma, Artha, Kama, Moksha and Bhakti. Fifth dimension indicates the need to recognize supreme power in this material world and devotion for him. These items were written based on the literature review of the several concepts like self, self-transcendence, ego-transcendence, within this work. These items were made to measure the perception of life satisfaction based on the selected dimensions with various aspects of life.

Selection of Raters: Twenty research scholars of psychology and twenty scholars of philosophy were selected to rate the initial 40 items draft of the scale for their appropriateness to measure life satisfaction. Based on a two-point scale to rate appropriateness "Yes or No" appropriate items were identified. These raters were provided an orientation cum training session to understand the purpose of the scale and its usability for measuring life satisfaction on the basis of Srimad Bhagavad Gita.

Rater Scoring: The raters scored the 40 items of the initial draft of the Life Satisfaction Scale for its appropriateness to measure life satisfaction. Each item was scored on a 5-point Likert scale ranging from 1 (strongly disagree) to 5 (strongly agree) in original format but raters were requested to mark each item as appropriate or inappropriate for measuring the dimension of life satisfaction.

Data Analysis: The scores of raters for appropriateness of the items to measure life satisfaction based on the principles of Gita were collected and analyzed using intraclass correlation coefficient (ICC) to determine the interrater reliability. ICC is a statistical method which is used to determine the degree of agreement between two or more raters as a structured agreement matrix and it is analyzed using statistical methods. After calculating the ICC, item analysis was conducted to identify the items consistently rated as appropriate for the purpose. Items with low agreements between raters were removed from the scale.

Development of the Final Draft: The items with low agreement were removed due to their inappropriateness to measure the life satisfaction as per the principles of the Srimad Bhagavad Gita. 10 items were removed from the initial draft of the life satisfaction scale which resulted in a final draft containing 30 items as given in the table.

Selection of Raters: The same 20 research scholars of psychology who rated the initial draft of the scale were selected to rate the final draft for the appropriateness for measuring life satisfaction based on Shriamd Bhagavad Gita principles. These research scholars were working on the intersection of Indian philosophy and psychology and had prior understanding of the core principles of Srimad Bhagavad Gita.

Rater Scoring: The raters again scored the 30 items in the final draft of the Life Satisfaction Scale for the appropriateness of the items to measure the related dimensions. The scale was drafted on a 5-point Likert scale ranging from strongly disagree to strongly agree.

Data Analysis: The given scores by selected raters were collected and analyzed using the intraclass correlation coefficient (ICC) to calculate the interrater reliability of the items in the final draft.

Interpretation of Results: The results of inter-rater reliability confirmed the statistical appropriateness of the scale model based on intraclass correlation coefficient (ICC). The interpretation of agreement between the raters provided evidence of agreement among the raters for measuring life satisfaction. The internal consistency of the results was investigated using Cronbach's alpha coefficient.

Chapter 21
Leadership Theories in Gita

Brief Review of Leadership Theories

Leadership is a complex and multifaceted concept due to its focus on motivating human behavior. The social and scientific progress of humans on this planet has been possible through the broader cooperation. This broader cooperation needs a connecting force which joins all the social actors. Widely researched in the field of organizational psychology and management, leadership has been explored through various theories of leadership which emphasize different aspects of effective leadership.

One of the latest theories of leadership is authentic leadership emphasizing the importance of self-awareness (which is emphasized as a first principle in Gita), transparency, and ethical behavior which is a core principle in Srimad Bhagavad Gita (Walumbwa, Avolio, Gardner, Wernsing, & Peterson, 2008). Authentic leaders are true to themselves and they understand their personal selves better. This inspires followers to also be authentic and true and committed to their work.

Another recent leadership theory, servant leadership focuses on leaders' role as servant to their followers (Greenleaf, 1970). By prioritizing the needs, aspirations, development of abilities and goals of their followers, servant leaders emphasize empowering their followers to attain their full potential which creates a positive and supportive work environment.

Leader-Member Exchange (LMX) theory is a recent development in leadership theoretical literature. It emphasizes the importance of the relationship between the leader and their followers which is supposed to be crucial for the phenomenon of leadership (Graen & Uhl-Bien, 1995). Leader-Member Exchange theory focuses on the phenomenon of leaders developing high-quality relationships with their followers to increase trust, loyalty and commitment in the team.

Bass and Riggio (2006) proposed the theory of transformational leadership that emphasizes the leader's role in inspiring and motivating followers to achieve shared goals. With Charisma, Vision and inspiration; Transformational leaders inspire followers to perform beyond the expectations and limitations for creating positive change.

Shared leadership emphasizes that leadership is distributed among team members as one of the latest theories (Pearce & Conger, 2003). It highlights the importance of collaboration, shared, decision-making, and communication among team members to achieve shared goals.

Positive leadership is a recent theory emphasizing the role of leaders in creating a positive work environment. This fosters well-being, happiness and meaningfulness (Cameron & Spreitzer, 2011). Positive leaders create a positive work culture by emphasizing positive emotions, resilience, and positive relationships among team members.

In conclusion, these theories of leadership provide unique frameworks and perspectives to analyze the properties of effective leaders. This has implications for guiding modules of leadership development and practice in various organizational contexts.

Transformational Leadership

Transformational leadership is a leadership style which focuses on achieving shared goals by inspiring and motivating team members for creating positive change in organizations (Bass, 1985). James McGregor Burns introduced the idea of transformational leadership during the 1970s as a process of empowering the colleagues for achieving higher potential and better team coordination (Burns, 1978). A plethora of research has been done on the topic of transformational leadership in various organizational outcomes.

Early studies focused on identifying the dimensions of the leadership style. Four dimensions were proposed by Bass (1985) as Charisma, inspirational motivation, intellectual stimulation and individualized consideration. Charisma refers to the ability of leaders to inspire the motivation and ability of others by personal characteristics and communication skills. Inspirational motivation is about creating a shared vision and setting high expectations by creating a shared vision to motivate followers. Intellectual stimulation is about setting a challenging landmark for followers to think in a creative and critical manner.

Subsequent research has investigated the impact of Transformational leadership on various organizational outputs. For example, Judge et al. (2002) found that transformational leadership is positively associated with job-satisfaction, organizational commitment, and job performance. Another meta-analysis by Wang et al (2013) found that transformational leadership was negatively related to turnover intention, thus helping in reducing the attrition rates in organizations.

Moreover, recent research investigated the mechanisms through which transformational leaders influence followers and organizations for example, Avolio and colleagues (2009) developed a mediation model based on the mediating role of psychological empowerment which is the ability of feeling in control of one's work and environment. This model proposes that transformational leadership promotes the feeling of psychological empowerment and transcends performance limitations. Zhang & Bartol (2010) examined its role in promoting creativity. Similarly Shin and Zhou (2007) studied the role of transformational leadership in promoting innovation in organizations.

In conclusion, transformational leadership has been studied extensively across disciplines over the past decades and the evidence of its effectiveness in producing positive organizational outcomes is documented. Future research could explore how organizational leadership can enhance the organizational culture, adaptation, strategic decision making in different organizational contexts and cultures, and how it can be developed and sustained over time.

Proposing a New Model of Leadership: Krishna Model of Leadership

This section proposes the Krishna Model of Leadership on the principles and teachings enshrined in the Srimad Bhagavad Gita, one of the most sacred Hindu scriptures. Based on the above literature reviews on the different aspects of Gita in all 18 chapters, this model is proposed here. Krishna is the central figure of the Bhagavad Gita who emerges as a great leader and teacher in Mahabharata war. His exposition of the reality and Dharma motivates Arjuna to take right decision. In the situation of crisis, a true leader provides direction by telling reality and providing accurate information. The Gita emphasizes self-awareness, self-reflection, self-restraint, ego-transcendence, and ethical behavior.

The Krishna Model of Leadership draws on and is based on these principles and linked theories of psychology in Gita. The broader theoretical framework of Gita which touches every domain of human behavior provides a comprehensive model of leadership. If we examine the influence of Gita it is related to personal cognitive, behavioral and ethical principles. Its scope extends to social behavior and duty as Karma and Purushartha. Beyond personal and social realms of life it deeply delves and anchors the spiritual understanding and development of human being. The ethical framework of Gita is essentialist which keeps the ethical behavior as foremost goal of life. An unethical behavior can't be justified beyond the Dharma. This model is unique and insightful representation of leadership providing a different perspective on leadership and can be a valuable tool for leaders in industry or education or social entrepreneurship.

Dimensions of Krishna Model of Leadership

Table 22: Dimensions of Krishna Model of Leadership

Serial No.	Dimension
1	Visionary leadership
2	Self-awareness and self-regulation
3	Decisiveness and commitment
4	Empowerment and delegation
5	Effective communication
6	Trustworthiness and integrity

Serial No.	Dimension
7	Humility and groundedness
8	Creativity and innovation
9	Gratitude and appreciation
10	Compassion and empathy
11	Learning mindset and continuous improvement
12	Ethical leadership and values-driven decision making

Visionary Leadership

Visionary leadership is a crucial dimension of leadership. It involves the use of ability to envision a compelling and realistic picture of the future for the society, organization or community. Vision is the futuristic dimension of leadership which is linked with common motivational factors which are necessary for maintaining the social thread and group cohesiveness in the community of followers for striving towards common ends. Several verses in Gita support this dimension of leadership.

In Bhagavad Gita Chapter 7 and Shloka 7, Lord Krishna says, "I am the source of all spiritual and material worlds and everything emanates from Me. "This verse emphasizes the importance of the interconnectedness of all things in the universe. A visionary leader should have a clear understanding of the organization's role and the duties of individual followers. A leader should understand the interconnecting and abiding interests of his group and find those principles which enhance interconnection and cooperation of the team. Above all a vision clarifies things for the followers and provides a clearer picture of his duties and prescribed results according to Dharma. Thus detached duty could only be performed if the direction, the future is clear. Krishna as a leader provides Arjuna a clearer picture of past, present, and future. He says that if you will win the war, you will become the king and if you lose, you will be said and remembered as a dutiful Kshatriya and would set an example for the society. Thus Krishna gives him both the options and guides him in giving a compelling vision of the future if he adheres to his prescribed duties by Dharma of a Kshatriya.

Shlokas in Bhagavad Gita highlight the transcendental nature of God and reality. Krishna, in several instances, mentions this fact. Chapter 9, Shloka 11 sheds light on the transcendental nature of reality and reincarnation of Krishna in human form. These verses highlight the importance of having a transcendent vision which shares the commonness and divinity of individual dignity. This helps in recognizing the potential for greatness in oneself and others. A visionary leader should be able to see beyond the current limitations and inspire the team towards a compelling vision.

Elon Musk, the CEO of Tesla and Space X has a visionary leadership style for holding vision for the future of sustainable energy and space exploration. Initially a difficult looking task was made possible by his efforts and envisioning of future in these areas. Now he has inspired thousands of people to join him in his mission. His leadership style is characterized by his ability to articulate a compelling vision of future in these unexplored areas and a relentless pursuit to fulfill it even in the face of adversity.

In summary, visionary leaders should have a clear understanding of the organizations role in the society and the larger scheme of industry and different stakeholders. He believes in the potential for greatness in oneself and others. They should be able to see beyond the present scenarios and understand the ongoing changes in the society and industry. Then only a compelling realistic and inspiring vision of future could be crafted which would be greater than what exists today.

Self-awareness and Self-regulation

Self-awareness and self-regulation are crucial dimensions of effective leadership in Gita. One who cannot control his senses can't regulate and control or guide others. Self-awareness help leaders manage their emotions and regulate them for broader goods of their team or society in large. The Bhagavad Gita provides several ways to address the lack of self-awareness and self-regulation at many instances in several verses which support this dimension of leadership.

Shloka 29 of Chapter 6 recalls us the one universal self, distributed in all beings, and presence of same self in all beings. One needs to understand and feel the presence of universal self of god in all beings (Gita 6.29).

Self-discovery in Gita highlights the importance of disciplined mind by the means of yoga and fixing it on inner reflection and introspection without any interference from outer physical and social worlds. Yoga is helpful in disciplining the body, mind and thought of person on the inner real self and basic desires which distract persons from their duties. The real self can be understood by means of reflection and focused contemplation about the real nature of existence (Gita 6.15)

Second chapter in Gita highlights the perennial and immortal nature of the human self which is unborn or never destroyed. It is unborn, perpetual and primeval. Self can be depicted as a microcosm of the macrocosm of universal self of god. It is situated in every human being and living being (Gita Chapter 8, Shloka 4). Self is seen as the major driving force in human life and if one can regulate and discipline the functions of self, then self can be his best friend. Otherwise, it is the worst enemy of the person which leads to the destruction of the destiny (Gita 6.6).

Controlling the mind and self is instrumental in retaining the calm in the situation of severe crisis. It gives peace and tranquillity, stability in the situation of crisis, pain, sorrow. A person can remain calm and controlled during the situation of honour and dishonour, if he has control over himself. Gita highlights the self as a stable immutable, imperishable entity beyond this physical world and connects it to the supreme self. The supreme self as per Srimad Bhagavad Gita is Shri Krishna (Chapter 6, Shloka 7). Supreme self is present in the heart and existence of all beings. Becoming self-content is one necessity in yoga and it helps in regulating the senses as per the prescribed duties in Dharma (Chapter 18, Shloka 61). Krishna is said to be the supreme yogi who exemplifies the condition of one supreme self, present in all beings. In the chapter 4, and shloka 18, the condition of action in inaction and inaction in action is explained. If Arjuna or any individual does action without attachment it would be inaction and its results would not be accumulated for giving rebirth and sorrow in life. The detached action as per the prescribed roles according to Dharma or duties of a leader, don't accumulate Karma and remains as a liberator force for him.

Acting of a leader detached and as per his prescribed duties or standard operating procedures liberates him, give satisfaction and frees from anxiety and conflicts. There is one another plausible reason of the verse which focuses on withdrawal from the duties. As Arjuna as a leader of Pandawas, fears to struggle and hesitate to raise his voice for the injustices done by Kaurawas; his duties of Kshatriya recalls him for a war. Krishna explains him that if you are withdrawing from your prescribed duties you are avoiding the prescribed Karmas which is a sin. Krishna elaborates to him that if a leader or individual doesn't fight against Adharma or sin, it is still a sin.

Decisiveness and Commitment

Decisiveness and commitment are crucial dimensions of leadership. These traits help leaders in making decisions in ambiguous, difficult and uncertain scenarios and follow through their plans in the face of adversity. Bhagavad Gita contains several instances where decisiveness and commitment are emphasized as dimensions of leadership.

In Bhagavad Gita, Chapter 2 and Shloka 47, Lord Krishna explains that an individual has the right to perform his duties as prescribed by Dharma or his organizational policies. The right to perform duties doesn't conform to the right of fruits or results of the task. It would be given by Dharma or may not result in desired outcomes but a person should never long for inaction. Thus it highlights the importance of commitment to individual's duties and work with a focus on process, rather than the outcome. A leader committed to his goals can inspire their followers by performing his duties detached and towards shared and compelling vision in the face of challenges.

In Bhagavad Gita, Chapter 3 and Shloka 19, Lord Krishna renunciates that detached action is a matter of duty and this is the way by which one can attain the supreme. A leader has to make the decisions in the face of challenges with the reference to his prescribed duties and not be influenced by personal gains and desires. A decisive leader is committed to perform his duties and inspire his followers with selflessness and detachment with the desired fruits and outcomes for acting in the service of greater good.

Elon Musk has demonstrated decisiveness and commitment as the CEO of SpaceX and Tesla. Apart from crafting a great vision for these corporates he had willingness to take risks in pursuit of his goals. Despite setbacks and challenges, he has remained committed to his vision of transforming transportation and space travel as an entrepreneur.

In summary a decisive and committed leader doesn't only take tough decisions in the face of uncertainty and adversity but also follows it relentlessly. Such leader who is committed to the goals and vision can inspire team members to work towards a shared vision.

Empowerment and Delegation

Empowerment and delegation are emphasized as important dimensions of leadership in Srimad Bhagavad Gita. Empowerment refers to the control of the factors which have potential to influence our lives and well-being. Similarly, delegation requires giving authority to individual and assigning responsibility. Several verses in Gita support this dimension of leadership.

In Bhagavad Gita chapter 18, Shloka 61, Lord Krishna says, "The supreme consciousness is situated in everyone's heart. He is directing the course of action of all living entities, who are designated as part of the larger whole. This highlights the idea that everyone has a unique role to play in the stage of world and each person is empowered to fulfill their role. A leader's role is to empower and clarify the factors which are required to succeed in work and focus on the goal. These factors are explaining the prescribed duties clearly and stimulating the intellectual capacities of the followers in order to empower them to critically analyze the situations of work and life. Individuals and followers should be motivated to understand that detached action as per the prescribed duty is the only key to success. Contemplating over goals and not taking action is a form of inaction and sin.

In Bhagavad Gita, chapter 3 Shloka, 3.27, Lord Krishna renunciates that soul is influenced by the sense of false ego and falsely thinks that it is the doer of activities and karma but they are carried out by different three modes of material nature- Sattva, Tamasa and Rajasa. This verse emphasizes that importance of recognizing that all actions are based on the divine will. Individuals need to know their true nature and concept of self and soul.

A leader who empowers his followers intellectually to understand their true nature, self, motivations of life and their ego can motivate them to follow shared goals with a detached perspective. When followers are more motivated by mere incentives and outcomes of the action, they compromise the prescribed duties, tasks and standard operating procedures.

In summary, empowerment and delegation are essential dimensions of effective leadership. They create a culture of trust and collaboration. It enables followers to work together as a team towards a common goal. A leader who empowers team members and delegates authority as per their nature is a successful leader. It leads to a greater level of cooperation, creativity and innovation within the group.

Effective Communication

Effective communication is an essential dimension of leadership. It involves conveying clear messages with clear intent to followers. Krishna as a teacher communicates to Arjuna clearly the essence of Dharma and Duty. Clearly and functional communication with colleagues and followers is a basic requirement of team formation and functioning,

The Bhagavad Gita provides several verses where clarity of communication is demonstrated by Krishna. When he explains his Virat Form – the grand reincarnation in Kurukshetra. He says and demonstrates clearly who is he, and makes it clear that all the beings are inside the Krishna The Bhagavad Gita provides several verses that can support this dimension of leadership.

Bhagavad Gita Chapter 9, Shloka 22 presents a relevant example of how a leader should communicate the goals, and incentives to the followers. Krishna says that a person who thinks about me all time, his all responsibilities are carried out by me. It's a kind of transcendental communication to the supreme which needs presence of pure mind and body. If a person becomes pure by mind and disciplined by body, most of the problems and sufferings are reduced to the minimum automatically. So it is a kind of silent communication where the heart of the devotee reaches out to God.

This verse also highlights the importance of surrendering to supreme as a form of spiritual communication where the devotee conveys trust and reliance on divine care. It's a communication of faith in the supreme. Krishna further assures in his response that – I provide what they lack and preserve what they have.

In Bhagavad Gita 2.47, Lord Krishna emphasizes upon performing prescribed duties in a detached manner but not expect the fruits of action. This verse also highlights that individuals has to perform his duties selflessly and inaction is a sin. Krishna communicates this fundamentals to Arjuna clearly and concisely. Thus, it is important for a leader to emphasize clear and concise communication to avoid misunderstanding and ambiguities for ensuring that their message is accurately conveyed.

Satya Nadella, the CEO of Microsoft can be considered a leader with effective communication skills. As a CEO, he has withstand the harsh competition and defined new benchmarks in the industry. His strategic decisions made in the sectors of cloud computing and artificial intelligence in 2024; and strategic partnerships and investments, particularly a substantial investment in artificial intelligence has given the firm new grounds and markets. Apart from these moves, he has focused on creating a culture of open communication at Microsoft, encouraging his employees to share ideas and collaborate across teams to maximize the culture of innovation and cooperative learning.

In summary, effective communication is a critical dimension of leadership as envisaged in Srimad Bhagavad Gita. It helps in enabling a strong relationship between leader and followers, fostering trust and respect. It also fosters trust and helps in avoiding misunderstanding. A leader who communicates clearly and sincerely can create a culture of open communication for encouraging creativity and innovation within the group.

Trustworthiness and Integrity

Trustworthiness and integrity as dimensions of an effective leadership foster honesty, transparency, and accountability in the team. The Bhagavad Gita provides several instances where trustworthiness, integrity are valued and this provides support for this dimension.

In Bhagavad Gita Chapter 17, Shloka 15, austerity of speech is emphasized. The austerity of speech is result of reflecting Vedic texts, disciplining mind. It helps in attaining truthfulness, coherence between the thought and action, leading to integrity. A leader should be trustworthy and honest. He should be capable of developing a sense of security and stability among his followers for fostering a culture of transparency and accountability.

In Bhagavad Gita 3.21, Lord Krishna explains the importance of the actions of great persons. They are followed by others and influence other people by their honesty and trustworthiness, integrity and transparency. A leader who demonstrates integrity and accountability can truly inspire their followers to do the same. It helps in creating a culture of trust and respect within the team and group.

A real-life example of a leader embodying trustworthiness and integrity in her personality is Indra Nooyi, the former CEO of the MNC PepsiCo Inc. During her tenure, Nooyi has emphasized the crucial role of honesty, integrity, accountability and trustworthiness in her leadership. This strategy encouraged her employees to speak up with necessary truth and innovations for product improvements. She has also worked for creating a culture of transparency at PepsiCo through regular communication and open dialogues at public forums between leaders and employees.

In summary, trustworthiness and integrity are critical dimensions of leadership, as they establish a sense of security and stability among followers, foster a culture of transparency and accountability, and inspire others to do the same. A leader who is honest, transparent, and accountable can create a culture of trust and respect, encouraging innovation and collaboration within the group.

Humility and Groundedness

Humility and groundedness are essential dimensions of leadership emphasized in Gita. It is named as *amanitvam* and is accepted as one of the central values which constitute true knowledge. It involves being humble, self-aware, and focused on the well-being of others as an essential attribute of wisdom and self-realization. In Srimad Bhagavad Gita, several verses support this dimension of leadership.

In Bhagavad Gita 13.8-12, Lord Krishna describes the qualities of a humble leader and person. A humble person has self-control, austerity, purity, forgiveness, and compassion towards others. The Bhagavad Gita sees humility as an essential aspect of knowledge and without it, true wisdom remains incomplete. It is developed through relationships and is not just a personal trait but a relational virtue which reflects in our interactions with others. Difficulties help us cultivate humility. A leader who is focused on the well-being of others is more likely to inspire, succeed and motivate their followers towards a shared goal.

Balancing humility and self-respect is essential, and in situations where someone is constantly dismissive and malicious, it is advisable to maintain a health distance. The ultimate purpose of humility is to align oneself for the service of supreme dwelling in all human being. A humble leader would selflessly act towards the welfare of the team and followers and provides a source of intrinsic motivation. A humble leader makes his team humble and accommodating for the maximum cooperation and results and creates a culture of inclusivity and respect within the group.

A real-life example of a leader embodying humility and groundedness is Satya Nadella, the CEO of Microsoft who emphasized the importance of empathy and humility in work world. He focused on building a culture of inclusivity, respect, humility and cooperation in Microsoft. By emphasizing the importance of cooperation, humility, and continuous professional development he made the organization more resilient to embrace new challenges and opportunities.

In summary, as critical dimensions of leadership, humility and groundedness establish a sense of empathy and inclusivity among followers. It also fosters a culture of respect and collaboration for achieving extraordinary goals and inspire others to embrace continuous learning and growth. A leader who is humble, self-aware, and focused on the well-being of others can gear changes which inspire to create a culture of innovation and creativity. He encourages followers to reach their full potential.

Creativity and Innovation

Creativity and innovation are essential dimensions of 21st century life skills and they are imperatives for the contemporary leaders to cherish with. They help in development of the ability to generate new ideas and solutions to the problems. In Bhagavad Gita, there are several verses supporting this dimension of leadership.

In Bhagavad Gita 10.41, Lord Krishna reminds Arjuna that whatever is splendid and beautiful in this world is his manifestation. It is a portion of his splendor and prowess. So, every uniquely endowed individual is manifestation of Krishna's abilities and a good leader should celebrate the unique talents and abilities of individuals within the group. Encouraging creativity and recognizing the unique talents of individuals in team can be real strategies to diversify and harness the talents to achieve extraordinary results.

In Bhagavad Gita 9.22, Lord Krishna explains that a person who is devoted to me and meditates on my transcendental form which is pervasive in all beings; is being taken care of by me. This verse has indirect implications for believing in individuals' abilities and having faith in oneself. Thus, a leader who believes in his abilities and creative potential of team members can maximize the outputs of team effort and inspire his followers to have confidence in their abilities, encouraging them to take risks and pursue their own creative ideas.

In summary, creativity and innovation are critical dimensions of leadership, focusing on inspiring followers to capitalize on their unique talents and abilities and to have faith in themselves and their ideas. This inspires them to transcend their own capacities and boundaries. A leader who encourages creativity and innovation and understands that each ability within an individual is the gift of God, respects the unique talents and abilities of the individuals and synchronizes them with the broader vision. Thus he becomes able in fostering a culture of collaboration, experimentation, and growth and an environment of continuous improvement and progress.

Gratitude and Appreciation

Gratitude and appreciation are essential dimensions of leadership in the Gita. A person has to recognize his own true self and should appreciate the presence of the Supreme in every human being. Appreciating the presence of divine in everything enables to be thankful for all aspects of life and challenges. The Bhagavad Gita provides several verses which shed light on the importance of gratitude as a major dimension of leadership.

In Bhagavad Gita Chapter 4, Shloka 33; Krishna emphasizes that the essence of yoga is to see the presence of one immutable undivided imperishable reality in all beings. This verse highlights the importance of understanding the connection among all beings and recognizing their inherent worth as part of the Supreme. A leader should understand the worth of team-members and respects their unique personalities and talents; attitude and qualities, positives and negatives with equanimity as a manifestation of God. By practicing this attitude, a leader remains effective in his decisions and fully capitalizes upon the diverse perspectives and contributions of all individuals.

In Bhagavad Gita Chapter 9 Krishna opens the secret of Bhakti. In starting of the discussion he assures Arjuna that he is the source and ultimate cause of the universe. There are manifestations of him in world. Krishna, despite not having any obligation to work, reincarnates himself for establishing good conduct and faith in Karma. The different manifestations are Brahm Loka, Deva Loka, Pitri Loka, Asur Loka and Mrityu Loka. As people behave and accumulate Karmas, they attain their different Lokas after death or continue to rebirth. Thus, as sole creator and destructor of this universe Krishna renunciates that a little offering made by love is acceptable to god. The feeling, the devotion and the Bhakti is stated as a means to liberation. The essence of Bhakti Yoga is unconditional, pure love to God.

In summary, gratitude and appreciation are critical dimensions of an enlightened individual—and especially a leader. Such leaders can inspire followers to feel esteemed, and can cultivate a sense of self-fulfillment, cooperation, and loyalty. A leader practicing gratitude and appreciation can create a culture of self-respect, mutual respect, inclusivity which values the diverse perspectives and contributions of all individuals. It fosters trust and mutual support.

Compassion and Empathy

Compassion and empathy are crucial for leaders involving that they understand their teammates and care for the wellbeing of followers. Without caring the wellbeing of individuals involved in the pursuit of common goals. The Bhagavad Gita provides discussion about it at several instances. These discussions can support this dimension of leadership.

In Bhagavad Gita 6.32, Lord Krishna says that one who sees me in all beings and all beings in me is not hidden from me and I am not hidden from me. Seeing Krishna in all beings makes a person sensitive and naturally responsible for the team. A leader practicing empathy and compassion is more apt to create a culture of care, concern, mutual respect valuing the wellbeing and dignity of all individuals.

In Bhagavad Gita Chapter 12, Shloka 13, Lord Krishna says that an individual friendly to all beings and is merciful, unattached, forgiving is dear to me. This verse emphasizes the importance of empathy, mercy, forgiveness for a leader. compassionate and empathetic leader can motivate their followers to have confidence and believe, thus fostering a sense of belonging and connection.

Scholars across various disciplines argue that students receive significant benefits when they are exposed to leadership models and methodologies, irrespective of the professional paths they eventually choose. Furthermore, integrating Social Emotional Learning (SEL) strategies into the educational landscape enriches leadership development and encourages personal growth through self-awareness and effective collaboration. Leadership is not solely derived from hierarchical authority but emerges from a reciprocal relationship of shared influence and mutual respect (Hammer, 2006). Consequently, individuals of all ages, backgrounds, and professional fields—ranging from sports and politics to education and community engagement—can demonstrate leadership (Welch & Welch, 2005). This includes fostering a sense of courage, openness to change, and an appreciation for cultural diversity. Schools must prioritize leadership development in their curriculum, ensuring that students are adequately exposed to leadership principles and real-world experiences. Failure to do so could leave students unprepared to navigate the complexities of modern society.

In summary, compassion and empathy are important factors in leadership able to foster a culture of care, concern, respect, and well-being, and dignity of all individuals. A leader who practices empathy and compassion can help the team members by personal consideration of their professional development and resource concerns for fully utilizing their potentials. This helps in fostering a sense of belonging and promotes a culture of kindness and understanding.

Learning Mindset and Continuous Improvement

The dimension of learning mindset and continuous improvement is essential for effective leadership and emphasized as critical component of several leadership models in literature of leadership. It involves having a growth-oriented mindset and a commitment to development of knowledge, skills and abilities of the leader and team members overall. It emphasizes creation of a collaborative learning environment where individuals support each other in their development and professional development. In the Bhagavad Gita several verses provide support for this dimension of leadership.

In Bhagavad Gita Chapter 4, Shloka 38; Lord Krishna says that knowledge is the most purifying thing in this world. This is knowledge by which a person gets rid of false ego and realizes the true self. Knowledge is instrumental in purifying the heart and mind and false ego. Thus, by a pure Chitta or mind, and resolute intelligence, a person can attain the true knowledge and salvation. This verse and other verses in this chapter emphasize the importance of getting knowledge and realizing oneself for development and social functioning. Knowledge also helps in understanding the duties and maintenance of a culture of growth and development.

In Bhagavad Gita Chapter 2, Shloka 70, Lord Krishna says that for attainment of peace, a person needs to give up all the desires by detachment, abstaining himself from egoism and the thirst for enjoyment. This verse emphasizes the importance of letting go of attachments and desires that hinder growth and development of individual. A leader practicing detachment and prioritizing growth over personal desires can inspire team members and promote a culture of continuous improvement.

A real-life example of a leader embodying a learning mindset and continuous improvement in industry sector is Satya Nadella (CEO of Microsoft). Nadella has emphasized the importance of ongoing learning and development during his tenure and thus equipped the organization with the capacity to adapt and evolve as per the needs of the industry and society. Microsoft Aspire Experience gives opportunity to employees to develop and enrich their skills for advancement of career. Understanding and valuing diverse perspectives is crucial for growth and development.

In summary, developing a mindset of continuous learning and development are essential dimensions of leadership in Gita. Krishna reiterates the importance of self-knowledge and self-reflection, discipline for a warrior and a leader. A leader who values these characteristics and can create a culture of growth and development, promoting continuous learning and progress.

In summary, a learning mindset and commitment to continuous improvement are essential dimensions of leadership, as they promote growth and development and inspire others to do the same. A leader who values ongoing learning and development contributes significantly to organizational success.

Ethical Leadership and Values-driven Decision Making

Gita has continuous emphasis on ethical behavior as prescribed by Dharma. This values-driven decision making becomes a crucial dimension, setting an example for followers for making decisions based on personal and organizational values, rather than personal gain. The Bhagavad Gita provides several verses supporting this dimension of leadership.

In Bhagavad Gita Chapter 3, Shloka 21, Lord Krishna says that the actions of great people are emulated by common people. They set examples for the society. That's why Krishna says in Gita that for the sustenance of societal functions, I reincarnate myself and engage in Karma. A leader upholding ethical principles and values can inspire their followers to follow the same conduct and promote a culture of ethical behavior.

In Bhagavad Gita 3.30, Lord Krishna says to Arjuna that a person with true knowledge without any attachment and without claims of proprietorship, without any lethargy would be able to perform his duties in best manner. This verse highlights the importance of making value-based decisions and upholding moral principles for inspiring their followers to act in similar ways for promoting a culture of integrity and ethical behavior.

Former CEO of Unilever, Paul Polman exemplified this by promoting a values-driven approach to leadership. He maintained continuous focus on sustainability, ethical behavior, and social responsibility. Under his leadership the corporate became a leader in sustainable business practices and made significant improvements in its environmental impact. Polman's ethical decision making and values-driven efforts set an example for the industry inspiring others to follow the same path for promoting a culture of ethical behavior within the organization.

In summary, ethical leadership and values-driven decision making are essential dimensions of leadership, as they promote a culture of integrity, moral principles, and ethical behavior. A leader who upholds ethical principles and values can inspire their followers to do the same, promoting personal and organizational success.

Krishna Model of Leadership Scale

The Krishna Model of Leadership Scale is a tool that measures the extent to which a leader embodies the personality characteristics of Lord Krishna based on different selected dimensions from the review. This scale consists of 22 items from 12 dimensions of the scale. For each item respondents are asked to rate each item on a five-point Likert scale ranging from "Never" to "Always".

The scale assesses different aspects of leadership such as

1. Visionary Leadership
2. Self-Awareness and Self-Regulation
3. Decisiveness and Commitment
4. Empowerment and Delegation

5. Effective Communication
6. Trustworthiness and Integrity
7. Humility and Groundedness
8. Creativity and Innovation
9. Gratitude and Appreciation
10. Compassion and Empathy
11. Learning Mindset and Continuous Improvement
12. Ethical Leadership and Values-Driven Decision-Making

The scale can be used to measure leadership qualities of individuals in alignment with the personality and behavioral traits of Shri Krishna. It can be applied across various industries, business, education, politics and social organizations. It can also be used to identify areas for improvement and enhancing performance. It can also be used for designing and developing training programs and training needs analysis.

The scale is developed on the basis of expert review using Delphi method and face validity has been established. It needs to be empirically validated on the basis of exploratory and confirmatory factor analysis.

This instrument provides a structured way to measure a new model of leadership based on Shri Krishna's personality and leadership traits. It is applicable across education, business, and other social organizations.

Table 23: Krishna Model of Leadership Scale

Dimension	S. No.	Item	Never	Rarely	Sometimes	Often	Always
Visionary leadership	1	Does the leader have a clear and compelling vision for the organization/team?					
	2	Do they inspire and motivate others to work towards this vision?					
Self-awareness and self-regulation	3	Does the leader understand their strengths and weaknesses?					
	4	Are they able to regulate their emotions and stay composed in challenging situations?					
Decisiveness and commitment	5	Does the leader make timely and effective decisions?					

Dimension	S. No.	Item	Never	Rarely	Sometimes	Often	Always
	6	Are they committed to achieving their goals and objectives?					
Empowerment and delegation	7	Does the leader empower others to take on responsibilities and make decisions?					
	8	Do they delegate tasks effectively?					
Effective communication	9	Does the leader communicate clearly and effectively?					
	10	Are they able to listen actively and respond appropriately to feedback?					
Trustworthiness and integrity	11	Does the leader act with honesty and integrity?					

Dimension	S. No.	Item	Never	Rarely	Sometimes	Often	Always
	12	Do they keep their promises and commitments?					
Humility and groundedness	13	Does the leader show humility and acknowledge their limitations?					
		Are they able to remain grounded and avoid getting carried away by their successes?					
Creativity and innovation	14	Does the leader encourage and foster creativity and innovation within the team/ organization?					
	15	Are they open to new ideas and approaches?					

Dimension	S. No.	Item	Never	Rarely	Sometimes	Often	Always
Gratitude and appreciation	16	Does the leader express gratitude and appreciation towards their team members?					
	17	Do they recognize and reward their team's achievements?					
Compassion and empathy	18	Does the leader show compassion and empathy towards others?					
	19	Are they able to understand and relate to others' perspectives?					
Learning mindset and continuous improvement	20	Does the leader have a growth mindset and strive for continuous improvement?					

Dimension	S. No.	Item	Never	Rarely	Sometimes	Often	Always
	21	Are they open to feedback and willing to learn from their mistakes?					
Ethical leadership and values-driven decision making	22	Does the leader make decisions that are consistent with ethical principles and values?					
	22	Do they prioritize the well-being of their team and stakeholders over personal gain?					

CHAPTER 22

Concept of Resolute Intelligence in Gita

In chapter 2, Shloka 55 of the Bhagavad Gita, Arjuna asks Lord Krishna to explain the behavior of Sthitprajna. According to Bal Gangadhar Tilak, Sthitprajna is the basis of Karmayogashastra. A person with Sthitprajna, is able to dispose all of his desires and remains self-content. Such person remains equipoised in favourable or unfavourable conditions. The dualism of pleasure and pain, heat and cold, and honor and dishonor cannot affect him. Further it is said that a person who is detached from desires, and anxiety of the desired or undesired outcomes can be called Sthitprajna. Withdrawal of senses from their subjects is a necessary condition. Not only withdrawal of senses is needed, the desire for them should also cease.

The importance of controlling senses is paramount for attaining the condition of Sthitprajna. A person who has controlled his senses can attain Sthitprajna. After controlling senses one has to live a disciplined life and devoted to God.

So a main characteristic of concept of sthitprajna or resolute intelligence is controlling senses and living a devoted and disciplined life. Apart from this Chapter 2, shlokas 62-65 the psychological process theory of desire and downfall of self is described. These shlokas systematically connect the psychological processes of human desire and suffering. Shloka 62 states that by continuously thinking about subjects or things, we get a desire for them. This shloka highlights the importance of perception and this is the starting point. Perception and continuous thinking of a subject introduces or causes desire. Fulfilment of this desire causes a temporary pleasure and consequent Karmas but if the desire is unfulfilled, it causes anger or frustration. Anger is itself a source of human suffering causing frustration and mental pain. This anger causes ambiguity or *bhram* (delusion). In this condition one is not able to make the right decision. Anger causes loss of memory and loss of decision-making ability. Loss of decision-making ability is the cause of ultimate destruction or downfall of a person.

If the person has resolute intelligence which is attained by the continuous practice of yoga by disciplining his mind and senses and developing a sense of detachment towards material desires. By following this path of self-control, control of desires, discipline and yoga one attains inner peace, self-realization, and ultimately, liberation from the cycle of birth, rebirth, suffering, and death.

The concept of resolute intelligence in the Bhagavad Gita emphasizes the importance of attaining a sound and stable mind which is free from the ego, transactions of senses and material desires, able to understand the difference between conscious purusha and material world as a deformity of the Prakriti. It teaches us to act with wisdom and detachment, and to cultivate a sense of equanimity towards all beings and to remain equipoised in adversities or difficult circumstances.

Literature Review on Resolute Intelligence

Resolute intelligence is a term that is not commonly used in academic literature. There are books as commentary of the Gita which explain the concept in detail. In empirical researches, this is closely related to emotional intelligence which is the ability to understand, control and manage emotions.

The term Sthitprajna is made of two terms – Sthita (Stable) and Prajna (Wisdom or intelligence). It signifies a person with unwavering wisdom, who remains unaffected by external circumstances and difficult situations. The ultimate goal of all sadhanas and spiritual disciplines is to achieve a still and unwavering mind. The unwavering mind is instrumental in attaining peace and tranquility by realization of the conscious soul which is indestructible and perennial. In Bhagavad Gita, Lord Krishna describes Sthitprajna as a person free from desire, detached and with a still mind. This concept is the very essence of Sadhana required for moksha or salvation.

Table 24 : Insights on Sthitaprajna (Resolute Intelligence) from Bhagavad Gita

Aspect	**Details**	**Shloka Reference (BG)**
Definition	A state of **stable wisdom**, where one is free from desires, attachments, fear, and disturbances, and remains **equanimous** in all situations.	2.55, 2.56

Aspect	**Details**	**Shloka Reference (BG)**
Characteristics	—Free from **desires** (Kama) —Unaffected by **joy and sorrow** —Detached from **fear, anger, and greed** — Firmly established in **Self-knowledge**	2.55, 2.56, 2.57
Sensory Control (Indriya Nigraha)	A Sthitaprajna withdraws the **senses from sense objects** like a tortoise withdrawing its limbs. This prevents distraction and stabilizes the mind.	2.58
Freedom from Desires	The sage renounces all **mental cravings** and finds **contentment within** the Self. Desires are seen as temporary and illusory.	2.55, 2.59
Mind's Stability	The mind remains **unshaken** even amidst disturbances, maintaining an **even vision** (Samadarshana) towards **success and failure**.	2.15, 2.57

Aspect	**Details**	**Shloka Reference (BG)**
Detachment (Vairagya)	True detachment is **not escapism** but being **in the world yet untouched by it**, like the **ocean remaining stable despite incoming rivers**.	2.70
Reaction to Praise & Criticism	A Sthitaprajna remains **unmoved** by honor or dishonor, neither elated by praise nor disturbed by blame.	12.19
Self-Sufficiency	Content in the **Self alone**, without seeking **external validation or material joy**.	2.55
Transcendence of Dualities	Sees **pleasure and pain, gain and loss, success and failure as the same**, thereby attaining **inner peace**.	2.15, 2.56
Control Over Emotions	— Does not react impulsively — Does not get **angry** (Krodha) — Has no **fear** (Abhaya) — No **attachment** (Raga)	2.56

Aspect	Details	Shloka Reference (BG)
Role of Wisdom (Jnana Yoga)	A **Sthitaprajna** possesses wisdom born from **Self-Realization** and is **firm in intellect** (Buddhi), unaffected by external distractions.	2.54, 2.72
Equality Towards All Beings	Treats **friends and enemies, rich and poor, joy and sorrow with an equal mind**.	12.19
Meditative Absorption (Samadhi)	Constantly **absorbed in Self-awareness**, even while performing worldly activities.	6.13
Liberation (Moksha)	A person of **stable wisdom** ultimately attains **liberation** (Brahmanirvana) by **realizing the Supreme Truth**.	5.20, 2.72
Final Instruction on Attaining Sthitaprajna	Renounce **ego** and **possessiveness**, remain **desireless**, and surrender to the **Supreme Lord** for ultimate peace.	2.71, 2.72

Sthiprajna is the ideal spiritual state for an individual. It is his duty to strive for attainment of this state. A person who achieves this state remains calm, composed and unaffected by sufferings of the life. For this, it is essential to eliminate distractions caused by worldly desires and attachments. The primary obstacle in spiritual progress is the wavering mind, which needs to be stabilized. Arjuna says to Krishna that mind is unstable and it remains engaged in subjects. So by means of yoga and control of senses a yogi stabilizes his mind. This is the primary necessity of the spiritual growth. Without Sthitprajna, one cannot attain Atma Jnana (Self-knowledge).

Major characteristics of a Sthitaprajna include freedom from desires or renouncement of desires. Inner contentment is the second trait which means a person needs to be self-satisfied and doesn't seek external pleasures. Even-mindedness in joy and sorrow is about treating happiness and misery with equanimity. Detachment from the worldly affairs and changes is another trait of Sthitprajna. Control over senses is depicted by a metaphor of tortoise which withdraws its limbs in its shell. Freedom from fear and anger arises from desires and by control of desires these emotions fade. Intellect of a Sthitprajna person remains steady and he is not swayed by external influences. The analogy of the ocean is used to explain the characteristics of a Sthitprajna person. Ocean remains stable despite the inflow of rivers. Similarly, the desires of the world continuously flow into the mind, but a stable person remains unaffected. Thus just as an ocean which is not affected by the inflow of rivers, a Sthitprajna remains unshaken despite worldly events.

In the context of the Bhagavad Gita, the concept of resolute intelligence is closely related to the practice of yoga and meditation. These help in individuals attaining higher levels of self-awareness and detachment from material desires. Empirical research has shown that practicing detachment and karmas can have a positive impact on mental health and can reduce symptoms of anxiety and improve overall well-being.

Difference Between Emotional Intelligence and Resolute Intelligence

Emotional intelligence (EI) and resolute intelligence (RI) are related concepts but they have some important differences. Sthitprajna is a state of stable wisdom where an individual is free from desires, fear, ego and is self-disciplined with complete inner peace and self-realization. On the other hand, emotional intelligence is the ability to recognize, understand, control and manage emotions for achieving greater inclusivity and personal and social well-being. Focus of Sthitprajna is to transcend emotions and achieve mental peace and liberation. Sthiprajna aims to overcome all emotions such as joy, sorrow, attachment, and anger while emotional intelligence theory explains the importance of emotions. It is based on the assumption that emotions are useful and manageable and could be used for navigating social and personal life effectively. They can help in achieving mental and social well-being. Emotional intelligence emphasizes self-regulation for expressing emotions in a constructive way without letting them control one's actions while Sthiprajna is a complete state of self-control where external situations or factors cannot disturb the internal equilibrium and peace. Sthitprajna helps in making decisions from pure wisdom based on Jnana which is free from biases and emotions while decisions from emotional intelligence are based on emotions and their balance. A Sthitprajna person would neither seek praise nor would be affected by criticism. He is undisturbed by praise or criticism. Emotionally intelligent person acknowledges praise and criticism but uses it for self-improvement and well-being.

In summary, emotional intelligence and resolute intelligence are related concepts but have different focuses when it comes to the final goal. Emotional intelligence function is control and regulation of emotions for well-being but Sthitprajna or resolute intelligence helps in attaining self-realization and complete withdrawal of emotions with an unwavering focus and steadfastness in the pursuit of one's goals and values despite external circumstances.

Verses Where Sthitaprajna or Resolute Intelligence is Mentioned in Gita and Their Interpretation

Bhagavad Gita, Chapter 2, Shloka 55, states that when one is able to withdraw the senses from their subjects, his intelligence is called resolute intelligence. This verse emphasizes the importance of withdrawal of senses from their respective subjects for practice of sensory detachment. The word Atman is used in this verse twice which indicates the individual self and supreme self.

Chapter 5, Shloka 20 mentions that a Sthitprajna person is not influenced by the transactions of senses. Just like an ocean which is not disturbed by the inflow of water from rivers, a person with resolute intelligence is not affected by the sensory inputs of senses. He remains undisturbed by the external influences and sensory attractions.

In Chapter 2, Shloka 56, mentions that an individual who is equipoised in sorrow and happiness, who is free from attachment, and anger, and is meditative in practice is called a person of resolute intelligence.

Chapter 2, Shloka 15 says that a person who is not affected by happiness and distress and remains steady in both is certainly Sthitprajna and qualified for liberation. This verse highlights the fact that remaining equanimous in happiness and distress is a characteristic of a Sthitprajna person. This verse says that for attainment of liberation, Sthitprajna is essential condition which frees a person from the bondage of birth and death.

Chapter 12 also highlights that a person who is equal to friends and enemies and is equipoised to honor and dishonor, heat and cold, happiness and distress and is satisfied and engaged in devotion to god as per the prescribed Dharma is a person of resolute intelligence. This kind of person is dear to God.

Chapter 6, Shloka 13 highlights the characteristics of a disciplined yogi who holds his neck, body and head erect and gazes at the tip of the nose during meditation without letting his mind and senses wander toward external subjects. This kind of person is having Sthitprajna or resolute intelligence and attains the state of samadhi. Physical and mental discipline in the practice of yoga is a fundamental necessity. For this a Yogi maintains discipline of the body in Samadhi and Pranayama. This substantiates the Yogic Philosophy which is aligned with Sankhya and Yoga philosophies.

Sthitprajna can be attained by practicing equanimity (Samatvam Yoga Uchyate, Bhagavad Gita, 2.48). Further, the Shloka 56 of chapter 2 states that a person who has attained Sthitprajna doesn't crave for worldly things and pleasures and remains free from all kinds of attachment.

Chapter 6, Shloka 2 states that true renunciation is not only giving up worldly possessions but also giving up the desires and attaining detachment. Swami Muktananda's commentary explains two types of Vairagya — Phalgu Vairagya which is indicative of people leaving worldly affairs but again fall back into attachment due to incomplete detachment. Yukta Vairagya or True renunciation is when one sees everything connected and dedicated to God, using it in His service rather than rejecting it outright. Sanyas or Vairagya needs Sthitprajna for becoming free from material desires, remaining absorbed in devotion to God, and maintaining the calm in external circumstances.

In Bhagavad Gita Chapter 2, Shloka 54, it is asked by Arjuna that what is the language of a Sthitprajna individual and how he behaves? The next shloka answers this by highlighting that when one gives up all desires arising in the mind and remains satisfied in the self then he attains steady wisdom.

Conclusion

In conclusion, the concept of Sthitprajna is an important aspect of the Bhagavad Gita. This concept plays an important role in all kind of Yoga. Karma Yoga, Jnana Yoga, Dhyan Yoga and Raj Yoga, and other kinds of Yogas are based on attainment of Sthitprajna. Without controlling senses and giving up the desires, one cannot attain equanimity, firmness, steadfastness, clarity of mind, and self-awareness. The attainment of Sthitprajna or resolute intelligence is necessary for spiritual enlightenment and liberation.

The various dimensions of resolute intelligence inferred from the verses of Srimad Bhagavad Gita are equanimity, firmness, steadfastness, detachment, self-awareness, clarity of mind.

Overall, the concept of Sthitprajna is a valuable reminder of the importance of developing a stable mind in order to navigate the challenges of life with wisdom, grace, and dignity for an individual. By cultivating it, we can find greater peace, happiness, and fulfillment.

Chapter 23

Principles of Andragogy in Srimad Bhagavad Gita

The Bhagavad Gita explains the situations where principles of adult learning or andragogy are indicated. Teaching Arjuna is itself an excellent example of andragogy where Krishna raises him from doubt to firm belief in Karma.

While the Gita is primarily a spiritual text about the theory of Karma and creation, it also contains valuable insights into the process of learning. The text naturally aligns with andragogical principles while it treats Arjuna as an adult learner. Gita respects autonomy of self-directed learning and draws upon experience of learner using past karma and knowledge. It connects learning to real-life problems by addressing the moral conflict in the war. It encourages self-inquiry rather than passive learning and focuses on reflection and application.

Table 25: Andragogy Principles in the Bhagavad Gita

Andragogy Principles	Application in the Bhagavad Gita
Self-Concept: From Dependency to Self-Direction	Krishna urges Arjuna to take responsibility for his own learning and realization. (**Gita 6.5**)

Andragogy Principles	Application in the Bhagavad Gita
Experience as a Resource for Learning	The Gita emphasizes that knowledge builds upon past karma and experiences. (**Gita 7.19**)
Readiness to Learn Based on Life Needs	Arjuna seeks Krishna's guidance only when he faces an existential dilemma. (**Gita 4.34**)
Orientation to Learning: Problem-Centered vs. Subject-Centered	Krishna provides practical wisdom that applies directly to Arjuna's situation. (**Gita 2.47**)
Motivation to Learn: Internal vs. External	True motivation for learning comes from within, not external rewards. (**Gita 6.8**)
Adults Need to be Involved in Planning and Evaluating Their Learning	Krishna encourages self-inquiry and independent reflection before deciding. (**Gita 18.63**)
Learning is Based on Experience (Including Mistakes)	Mistakes are part of learning and do not prevent spiritual progress. (**Gita 9.30**)
Adults Learn Best When Learning is Relevant to Their Lives	Knowledge in the Gita is immediately applicable to real-life concerns. (**Gita 2.48**)
Adult Learning is Problem-Centered Rather than Content-Oriented	Krishna tailors his teachings to Arjuna's immediate moral and ethical problems.

Malcolm Knowles' (1984) principles of andragogy and five assumptions can be mapped onto key teachings of the Gita.

Assumptions of Andragogy in the Gita

Evolving Self-concept from dependency to Self-Direction

Knowles emphasizes the importance of being self-directed learner from being a dependent learner. The Gita highlights the importance of Svadharma (One's own duty) and Atmajnana (Self-knowledge). The individual with self-knowledge can decide the best path of action as prescribed by the Dharma. Further in Shloka 5 of Chapter 6, says that only self can liberate itself (Uddhared Atmanatmanam). It aligns with the assumption of self-directed learning and taking responsibility for one's own actions and experiences

Experience as a resource of learning

Knowles states that adult learning is rooted in prior experiences and builds upon them. One has to take stock of the prior learning and experiences which learners bring with them. The Gita also emphasizes the role of one's past karmas and samskaras (Impressions) which shape one's present learning and actions. It highlights the importance of smriti (memory or recollection of experiences) in taking right decisions.

Readiness to learn based on life needs

Knowles asserts that adults learn when they perceive a need for knowledge to apply in a real-life situation or crisis. Until the need is felt, adults don't learn. Similarly, Gita illustrates how Krishna teaches Arjuna the spiritual path of Karma when he is in the most need during the moral crisis in war. Krishna doesn't force knowledge upon Arjuna but allows him to inquire according to his curiosity and the needs of the situation.

Learner Centric

Knowles states that adults focus on solving problems rather than accumulating knowledge. Gita also consistently emphasizes the importance of actions upon passive knowledge. Even Lord Krishna sets example by reincarnating himself to solve the problems of the world, as and when needed. For Lokasangrah (Survival of society) the God himself engages in the prescribed duties by reincarnation.

Intrinsic Motivation to Learn

Knowles emphasizes on intrinsic motivation to learn. External factors cannot make a sustainable learning effort and result. Until one is motivated to learn intrinsically and enjoys the process of learning, one cannot effectively learn. The Gita highlights that Self-Knowledge and liberation are the highest goals and true motivation comes towards the curiosity to attain self-realization.

Adults need to be involved in planning and evaluating their learning

The Gita doesn't give rigid dogmas but encourages self-inquiry and personal exploration to achieve true knowledge and wisdom. Krishna gives ample opportunity to self-reflect and decide for himself. In chapter 18, shloka 63, he says you have heard my teachings, reflect upon it and decide by your own what is right and wrong for you. Further he says that only you can liberate yourself, therefore, act accordingly.

Learning is based on experiences and mistakes

Krishna highlights that mind is not stable and even the wise make mistakes but by consistent disciplining of mind and practicing yoga, even the sinful can attain wisdom by seeking it sincerely (Chapter 9, Shloka 30).

Learning should be relevant to the lives of learner

Gita is not theoretical but it is a call to action in the situation of war, life and death. It applies to daily life, work, relationships, and challenges. Krishna provides practical wisdom that is immediately applicable, such as samatvam yogam uchyate (Gita, Chapter 2, Shloka 48).

Adult learning is problem-centred not only content oriented

As Knowles states that adults learn best when they use the knowledge and learning to solve real life problems, rather than memorizing for status or show off. The Gita itself begins with Arjuna's problems of fighting in the war. Krishna inspires him to act according to the different paths available to Karma Yogis and decide his own course of action.

Active Participation

Active participation is also one of the most important principles of learning that can be gleaned from the Gita. Krishna advises Arjuna to act according to his nature and decision as per his own Dharma in order to learn and grow. This idea is similar to the concept of active participation in modern learning theories.

Another important principle of learning that can be found in the Gita is the value of reflective practice. Krishna encourages Arjuna to reflect on his actions and their consequences, and to use this reflection to inform his future decisions. This emphasis on self-reflection and introspection is similar to the idea of reflective learning in modern educational theory, which emphasizes the importance of metacognition and self-awareness in the learning process.

The Gita also emphasizes the importance of self-directed learning. Krishna urges Arjuna to act according to his own nature and dharma, rather than merely following the dictates of others. This idea is similar to the concept of self-directed learning in andragogy, which is the theory of adult learning. Self-directed learning involves taking responsibility for one's own learning, setting goals, and identifying strategies for achieving them.

Finally, the Gita emphasizes the importance of learning through experience. Krishna tells Arjuna that he must act in the world in order to learn and grow, and that this learning is more meaningful than any external reward or outcome. This emphasis on experiential learning is similar to the concept of learning by doing, which is central to many modern theories of learning.

In conclusion, the Bhagavad Gita provides valuable insights into the process of learning through different principles and assumptions. Principles of active participation, reflective practices, self-awareness, self-directed learning and experiential learning are applied in Gita. By studying the teachings of the Gita, we can deepen our understanding of our learning process and decision-making for the betterment of our own lives.

Summary

The present study aimed to explore the principles of psychology which could be applied to present learning scenarios. Indian culture is perennial and a continuous entity. As one of the most ancient cultures of the world, it has philosophies and great epics as heritages. These philosophies and sacred texts contain ancient wisdom which are obtained from disciplined life and Yoga. These are derived from experiments of sages on their own bodies as Tapas. This austerity and hard discipline has resulted into the practices and principles of life which are indicated in the Srimad Bhagavad Gita. As part of prasthantrayi, this text contains several psychological principles in it.

Chapter 1 provided an introduction to the study by highlighting the importance of Srimad Bhagavad Gita as a source of wisdom and guidance for individuals across generations and different sectors of business, education and social organization.

Chapter 2 presented a systematic literature review and bibliometric analysis of researches on Gita. It also presents an overview of current literature of psychological research on the topic of educational psychology in Gita and provides a theoretical framework for the study.

Chapter 3 focused on the research methodology used in this study. Based on the conceptual review of the Srimad

Bhagavad Gita, the methodology uses an inductive framework. It applies juxta-positioning the concepts of Gita with modern psychology and educational psychology.

Chapter 4 includes deliberation on the principles of educational psychology applied in the context of Srimad Bhagavad Gita. Knowledge is said to be of utmost importance and self-purifying in the Gita. The text emphasizes the importance of self-awareness, self-regulation, self-reflection, ego transcendence, self-transcendence, mindfulness, resilience, perseverance and authenticity. The psychological process theory of desire is also explained in it. This theory highlights the importance of perception in causing desire which causes anger resulting in the loss of memory and wisdom and finally leading to downfall of the individual. Principles of emotional intelligence, mindfulness, self-compassion, self-acceptance, interconnectedness and self-reflection are discussed and their importance is stated in personal growth and development.

Development of psychological tools was an objective of this study. This study reviews the present literature on leadership relevant to educational scenarios and then explores the wisdom of Gita resulting in a twelve dimensions instrument to measure Krishna Model of Leadership.

Finally, the study examined the assumptions and principles of andragogy in the context of Gita. Arjuna as n learner embodies the perfect example of an adult learner who is in the need of true guidance from Krishna. This study outlines the principles and assumptions as per the Gita.

Overall, the study contributes to the growing body of research on the Srimad Bhagavad Gita on the intersection of psychology and spirituality. The findings of the study suggest that Srimad Bhagavad Gita offers a rich understanding of the psychological processes and entities. It explains how the intelligence is born as a deformity of the Prakruti by the influence of Purusha. Then it leads to ego and a false understanding of the self which is pure conscious and immutable. This false understanding leads to the unwise karmas and ahankaras (ego). It also explains the psychological process of desire as a theory. The development of psychological tools based on Gita and the proposed Krishna Model of Leadership have the potential to contribute to designing better curricula and training programs.

Implications of the Research

The study offers an alternative indigenous perspective on educational psychology. With the rise of indigenous knowledge systems worldwide and their recognition through decolonization efforts from Eurocentric perspectives Indian educational system needs a fresh revival away from Western behavioral and mechanistic perspectives on learning. The concept of man as visualized in NEP and Indian scriptures is more holistic than that of Western psychology which is fragmented and presents often contradictory views. Thus, this study presents an overview of educational psychology based on Indian concept of human beings. It offers fresh perspectives, assumptions, principles and theories of learning and personality. Principles of emotional intelligence, mindfulness, self-awareness, self-regulation, perseverance, authenticity, self-compassion, and self-transcendence present in Gita can offer numerous practical guidelines for designing educational curricula and training programs and can contribute to personal growth and development.

Development of psychological tools: The development of psychological tools, such as the Life Satisfaction Scale and the Krishna Model of Leadership Scale, and emotional intelligence, resolute intelligence based on the Gita has important implications for contemporary world, educators and leaders. These tools further could be validated psychometrically and used to enhance the quality of education and a better Indian society which is rooted in its cultural heritage and way of thinking.These tools can also be used to measure and promote personal growth, training needs assessment, designing tailored training programs based on analysis, to enhance well-being among individuals and adaptability in organizations.

Leadership development: The study proposes the Krishna Model of Leadership, based on the learnings from Gita. This model proposes a 12 dimensions scale with dimensions of 1. Visionary Leadership, 2. Self-Awareness and Self-Regulation, 3. Decisiveness and Commitment, 4. Empowerment and Delegation, 5. Effective Communication, 6. Trustworthiness and Integrity, 7. Humility and Groundedness, 8. Creativity and Innovation, 9. Gratitude and Appreciation, 10. Compassion and Empathy, 11. Learning Mindset and Continuous Improvement, and 12. Ethical Leadership and Values-Driven Decision-Making. Furthermore, the study also proposes a 22-items scale to measure the leadership.

Cross-cultural applications: The principles of educational psychology identified in this study have cross-cultural applications in the aspect that they can be universally applied and examined. As essence of one of the most ancient living cultures, these insights from Gita, enable us to examine the authenticity of our lives in the contemporary age. It also offers implications for individuals and organizations seeking transformative and positive changes, personal growth and development across cultures.

Integration with modern psychology: The study highlights the potential benefits of integrating ancient spiritual practices with modern psychological practices for better outcomes, such as in cognitive-behavioral therapy or positive psychology. It can offer significant implications for individuals and organizations seeking to promote growth in a sustainable, holistic and integrated manner.

In conclusion, this research has important implications for educational psychology, personal growth and development, leadership development, cognitive-therapy and integration of spiritual practices with modern psychological principles. The study contributes to a greater understanding of personality, leadership, learning styles, mindfulness, and other relevant applied psychological principles. It provides a foundation for further empirical and experiential research in this area.

Comparative Study: One potential avenue in this area is to conduct a comparative study of the principles of educational psychology across spiritual texts across the cultures and spiritual practices. Such a study would help in providing empirical and documentary evidence about the effectiveness of these principles of Gita. It would also identify commonalities and differences between spiritual traditions and to explore the implications of these differences for personal growth, wellbeing, mindfulness, peace, tranquility, liberation, personal growth and development.

In summary there is still a need for further empirical research based on the principles and theories derived from Shriamd Bhagavad Gita. These insights can be of significant use for educational psychology and leadership. The suggestions outlined above provide a foundational discourse on the empirical utility, practical application and provide a starting point for future research in this area.

Reference

1. Adams, L. J., MacLean, R. R., Portnoy, G. A., Beauvais, J., & Stacy, M. A. (2022). Psychology trainee and supervisor perspectives of multicultural supervision. *Psychological Services, 20* (S1), 78–85. https://doi.org/10.1037/ser0000643

2. Adi Shankaracharya. *Commentaries on the Bhagavad Gita* (translations vary; e.g., Swami Gambhirananda (1984), Advaita Ashram).

3. Adler, M., Cherniss, C., Goleman, D., Emmerling, R., & Cowan, K. (1998). *Bringing emotional intelligence to the workplace: A technical report issued by the Consortium for Research on Emotional Intelligence in Organizations.* Retrieved from https://www.researchgate.net

4. Akhurst, J. (2020). A South African perspective on community psychology practice competencies. *Journal of Community Psychology, 48*(6), 2108–2123. https://doi.org/10.1002/jcop.22410

5. Avolio, B. J., Walumbwa, F. O., & Weber, T. J. (2009). Leadership: Current theories, research, and future directions. *Annual Review of Psychology, 60*, 421–449.

6. Baker, Z. G., Tou, R. Y., Bryan, J. L., & Knee, C. R. (2017). Authenticity and well-being: Exploring positivity and negativity in interactions as a mediator. *Personality*

and Individual Differences, 113, 235–239. https://doi.org/10.1016/j.paid.2017.03.018

7. Bakosh, L. S., Snow, R. M., Tobias, M. J. M., Houlihan, J. L., & Barbosa-Leiker, C. (2016). Maximizing mindful learning: Mindful awareness intervention improves elementary school students' quarterly grades. *Mindfulness, 7,* 59–67. https://doi.org/10.1007/s12671-015-0387-6

8. Bar-On, R. (2004). The Bar-On Emotional Quotient Inventory (EQ-i): Rationale, description and summary of psychometric properties. In G. Geher (Ed.), *Measuring emotional intelligence: Common ground and controversy* (pp. 115–145). Nova Science Publishers.

9. Bass, B. M. (1985). *Leadership and performance beyond expectations*. Free Press.

10. Bass, B. M., & Riggio, R. E. (2006). *Transformational leadership* (2nd ed.). Lawrence Erlbaum Associates.

11. Baumeister, R. F., Vohs, K. D., & Tice, D. M. (2007). The strength model of self-control. *Current Directions in Psychological Science*, 16(6), 351–355. https://doi.org/10.1111/j.1467-8721.2007.00534.x

12. Beardslee, W. R. (1989). The role of self-understanding in resilient individuals: The development of a perspective. *American Journal of Orthopsychiatry*, 59(2), 266–278.

13. Bernard, M. E. (Ed.). (2013). *The strength of self-acceptance: Theory, practice, and research.* Springer Science+Business Media. https://doi.org/10.1007/978-1-4614-6806-6

14. Bhagavad Gita. (n.d.). In various translations and commentaries (e.g., Prabhupada, A. C. B. S., 1986; Zaehner, R. C., 2023; Ranganathananda, S., 2021). Verses cited throughout the text.

15. Bhagavad Gita (Translation and Commentary). Various verses quoted and analyzed. (Original Sanskrit text).

16. Bhawuk, D. P. S. (2008). Globalization and indigenous cultures: Homogenization or differentiation? *International Journal of Intercultural Relations, 32*(4), 305–317. https://doi.org/10.1016/j.ijintrel.2008.06.002

17. Bilgrami, A. (2011). Gandhi's religion and its relation to his politics. In *The Cambridge Companion to Gandhi* (pp. 93–116). https://doi.org/10.1017/CCOL9780521116701.006

18. Bird, J., & Caligor, E. (2024). A case report of the treatment of narcissistic personality disorder with transference-focused psychotherapy. *Journal of Clinical Psychology, 80*(5), 1177–1191. https://doi.org/10.1002/jclp.23637

19. Blanchard, K., & Jackson, A. (2006). *The leadership process: Learning, leading, and influencing.* New York: Wiley.

20. Block, J. H., & Block, J. (1980). The role of ego-control and ego-resiliency in the organization of behavior. In W. A. Collins (Ed.), *Minnesota symposia on child psychology* (Vol. 13, pp. 39–101). Lawrence Erlbaum Associates.

21. Bluth, K., & Blanton, P. (2015). The influence of self-compassion on emotional well-being among early and older adolescent males and females. *Journal of Positive Psychology, 10*(3), 219–230. https://doi.org/10.1080/17439760.2014.936967

22. Bluth, K., Park, J., & Lathren, C. (2020). Is parents' education level associated with adolescent self-compassion? *Explore, 16*(4), 225–230. https://doi.org/10.1016/j.explore.2020.02.003

23. Bouche-Florin, L., Skandrani, S. M., & Moro, M. R. (2007). La construction identitaire chez l'adolescent de parents migrants. *Santé mentale au Québec, 32*(1), 213–227. https://doi.org/10.7202/016517ar

24. Brandtstädter, J., & Renner, G. (1990). Tenacious goal pursuit and flexible goal adjustment: Explication and age-related analysis of assimilative and accommodative strategies of coping. *Psychology and Aging, 5*(1), 58–67.

25. Brown, K. W., & Ryan, R. M. (2003). The benefits of being present: Mindfulness and its role in psychological well-being. *Journal of Personality and Social Psychology, 84*(4), 822–848. https://doi.org/10.1037/0022-3514.84.4.822

26. Budianto, P. (2019). Foreignization and domestication strategies in Indonesian translations of *Tao Te Ching*. *Litera*. Universitas Negeri Yogyakarta. https://doi.org/10.21831/ltr.v18i2.25218

27. Bürgy, M. (1997). Self-reflection, interpersonal behavior and psychoanalytic ethics. *Psychotherapie Psychosomatik Medizinische Psychologie, 47*(5), 181–186.

28. Burns, J. M. (1978). *Leadership*. Harper & Row.

29. Cameron, K. S., & Spreitzer, G. M. (Eds.). (2011). *The Oxford handbook of positive organizational scholarship*. Oxford University Press.

30. Cantril, H. (1965). *The pattern of human concerns.* Rutgers University Press.

31. Cartwright, G. F., Tabatabai, D., Beaudoin, M.-C., & Naidoo, L. (2000). Self-actualization of youth in a summer camp. *Psychological Reports, 87*(3), 729–730. https://doi.org/10.2466/pr0.2000.87.3.729

32. Chatterjee, D. (2024). A critical analysis of the psychological concepts in the Bhagavad Gita. *Journal of Indian Psychology, 15*(3), 122-135. Available at SSRN: https://ssrn.com/abstract=4815485

33. Chen, J. (2020). Study on back translation of *Tao Te Ching*: The Taoism of Lao Tzu explained by Stefan Stenudd. *Advances in Social Science, Education and Humanities Research*. Atlantis Press. https://doi.org/10.2991/assehr.k.201215.467

34. Cloninger, C. R. (2004). Feeling good: The science of well-being. New York, NY: Oxford University Press.

35. Crowne, D. P., & Marlowe, D. (1961). A new scale of social desirability independent of psychopathology. *Journal of Consulting Psychology, 24*(4), 349–354. https://doi.org/10.1037/h0047358

36. D'Argembeau, A., Feyers, D., Majerus, S., Collette, F., Van der Linden, M., Maquet, P., & Salmon, E. (2008). Self-reflection across time: Cortical midline structures differentiate between present and past selves. *Social Cognitive and Affective Neuroscience, 3*(3), 244–252. https://doi.org/10.1093/scan/nsn020

37. Deci, E. L., & Ryan, R. M. (2000). The "what" and "why" of goal pursuits: Human needs and the self-determination of behavior. *Psychological Inquiry, 11*(4), 227–268. https://doi.org/10.1207/S15327965PLI1104_01

38. DeNeve, J. E. (2011). Functional polymorphism (5-HTTLPR) in the serotonin transporter gene is associated with subjective well-being: Evidence from a U.S. nationally representative sample. *Journal of Human Genetics, 56*(6), 456-459. https://doi.org/10.1038/jhg.2011.39

39. Dewey, J. (1938). *Experience and education*. Macmillan.

40. Diener, E. (2000). Subjective well-being: People's cognitive and affective evaluations of their lives. In E. Diener (Ed.), *Culture and subjective well-being* (pp. 34–36). MIT Press.

41. Diener, E., & Chan, M. Y. (2011). Happy people live longer: Subjective well-being contributes to health and longevity. *Applied Psychology: Health and Well-Being, 3*(1), 1–43. https://doi.org/10.1111/j.1758-0854.2010.01045.x

42. Diener, E., & Chan, M. Y. (2011). Happy people live longer: Subjective well-being contributes to health and longevity. *Applied Psychology: Health and Well-Being, 3*(1), 1–43.

43. Diener, E., & Diener, M. (1995). Cross-cultural correlates of life satisfaction and self-esteem. *Journal of Personality and Social Psychology, 68*(4), 653–663. https://doi.org/10.1037/0022-3514.68.4.653

44. Diener, E., & Seligman, M. E. P. (2002). Very happy people. *Psychological Science, 13*(1), 81–84.

45. Diener, E., Emmons, R. A., Larsen, R. J., & Griffin, S. (1985). The satisfaction with life scale. *Journal of Personality Assessment, 49*(1), 71–75. https://doi.org/10.1207/s15327752jpa4901_13

46. Diener, E., Emmons, R. A., Larsen, R. J., & Griffin, S. (1985). The Satisfaction with Life Scale. *Journal of Personality Assessment, 49*(1), 71–75.

47. Diener, E., Kahneman, D., Tov, W., & Arora, R. (2010). Income's association with judgments of life versus feelings. In E. Diener, J. F. Helliwell, & D. Kahneman (Eds.), *International differences in well-being* (pp. 3–15).

Oxford University Press. https://doi.org/10.1093/acprof:oso/9780199732739.001.0001

48. Diener, E.; Oishi, S., & Tay, L. (2012). Advances in subjective well-being research: The "new science" of happiness and flourishing. *Psychological Science in the Public Interest, 13*(1), 105-124. https://doi.org/10.1177/1529100612455614

49. Diener, E., Oishi, S., & Tay, L. (2018). Advances in subjective well-being research. *Nature Human Behaviour, 2*(4), 253–260.

50. Diener, E., Sapyta, J. J., & Suh, E. (1998). Subjective well-being is essential to well-being. *Psychological Inquiry, 9*(1), 33–37.

51. Doris, J. M. (2016). Précis of Talking to Our Selves: Reflection, Ignorance, and Agency. *Behavioral and Brain Sciences, 41*, e36. https://doi.org/10.1017/S0140525X16002016

52. Dryden, W., & Still, A. (2006). Historical aspects of mindfulness and self-acceptance in psychotherapy. *Journal of Rational-Emotive & Cognitive-Behavior Therapy, 24*(1), 3–28. https://doi.org/10.1007/s10942-006-0026-1

53. Easwaran, E. (2007). *The Bhagavad Gita for daily living*. Nilgiri Press.

54. Egan, H. H., Keyte, R., McGowan, K., Peters, L., Lemon, N., Parsons, S., Meadows, S., Fardy, T., Singh, P., & Mantzios, M. (2018). 'You before me': A qualitative study of healthcare professionals' and students' understanding and experiences of compassion in the workplace. *Health Professions Education, 4*(3), 149–159. https://doi.org/10.1016/j.hpe.2018.04.001

55. Elder, J., Cheung, B., Davis, T., & Hughes, B. (2023). Mapping the self: A network approach for understanding psychological and neural representations of self-concept structure. *Journal of Personality and Social Psychology, 124*(2), 237–263. https://doi.org/10.1037/pspa0000315

56. Erikson, E. H. (1982). The life cycle completed. New York, NY: Norton.

57. Faith, L. A., Wiesepape, C. N., Bonfils, K. A., Lysaker, P. H., & Schnakenberg Martin, A. M. (2024). Psychotherapy to emphasize self-directed recovery for persons with serious mental illness: Contributions from metacognitive reflection and insight therapy (MERIT). *Psychological Services, 21*(4), 928–937. https://doi.org/10.1037/ser0000865

58. Feezell, R. (2013). Sport, philosophy, and good lives. *Sport Philosophy and Good Lives* (pp. 1–272).

59. Feuerstein, G. (2011). *The Bhagavad Gita: A new translation*. Shambhala Publications.

60. Frankl, V. E. (1963). Man's search for meaning: An introduction to logotherapy. New York, NY: Washington Square Press.

61. Fuentes-Claramonte, P., Martin-Subero, M., Salgado-Pineda, P., Santo-Angles, A., Argila-Plaza, I., Salavert, J., ... & Salvador, R. (2019). Brain imaging correlates of self- and other-reflection in schizophrenia. *NeuroImage Clinical, 25*, 102134. https://doi.org/10.1016/j.nicl.2019.102134

62. Fujita, F., & Diener, E. (2005). Life satisfaction set point: Stability and change. *Journal of Personality and Social Psychology, 88*(1), 158–164. https://doi.org/10.1037/0022-3514.88.1.158

63. Gao, M. (2020). On the cultural dissemination of *Tao Te Ching* in the western world. *OALib*. Scientific Research Publishing. https://doi.org/10.4236/oalib.1106018

64. Garcia, D., Anckarsäter, H., & Cloninger, C. R. (2014). Resilience in adolescence through positive emotions and self-transcendence. Comprehensive Psychiatry, 55(3), 586-592.

65. Garg, R. (2019). Resilience in the Bhagwadgita: A discourse analysis. *International Journal of Indian Psychology*, 7(4), 789–794. DOI: 10.25215/0704.090

66. Graen, G. B., & Uhl-Bien, M. (1995). Relationship-based approach to leadership: Development of Leader-Member Exchange (LMX) theory over 25 years. *The Leadership Quarterly, 6*(2), 219–247.

67. Grant, S., Langan-Fox, J., & Anglim, J. (2009). The Big Five traits as predictors of subjective and psychological well-being. *Psychological Reports, 105*(1), 205–231. https://doi.org/10.2466/PR0.105.1.205-231

68. Greenberg, M. T., Weissberg, R. P., O'Brien, M. U., Zins, J. E., Fredericks, L., Resnik, H., & Elias, M. J. (2003). Enhancing school-based prevention and youth development through coordinated social, emotional, and academic learning. *American Psychologist, 58*(6-7), 466.

69. Greenleaf, R. K. (1970). *The servant as leader*. Robert K. Greenleaf Center.

70. Hammer, K. (2006). Leadership development: Creating a culture of leadership. *Academic Leader, 22*(2), 7-8.

71. Handler, R. (1986). Authenticity. *Anthropology Today, 2*(1), 2–4. https://doi.org/10.2307/3032899

72. Hayes, S. C., Strosahl, K. D., & Wilson, K. G. (2006). *Acceptance and commitment therapy: An experiential approach to behavior change*. Guilford Press.

73. Helliwell, J. F. (2007). Well-being and social capital: Does suicide pose a puzzle? *Social Indicators Research, 81*(3), 455–496. https://doi.org/10.1007/s11205-006-0022-2

74. Helliwell, J. F. (2008). Life satisfaction and quality of development (NBER Working Paper No. 14507). National Bureau of Economic Research.

75. Helliwell, J. F., Layard, R., & Sachs, J. (Eds.). (2013). *World Happiness Report 2013*. Sustainable Development Solutions Network.

76. Henderson, Z., Kia-Keating, M., & Woods-Jaeger, B. (2023). Reimagining traumatic stress studies as a participatory science grounded in critical self-reflection: A call to action. *Journal of Traumatic Stress, 36*(4), 665–667. https://doi.org/10.1002/jts.22952

77. Herling, B. L. (2005). The German Gita: Hermeneutics and discipline in the German reception of Indian thought, 1778–1831. *The German Gita: Hermeneutics and Discipline in the German Reception of Indian Thought, 1778–1831*. https://doi.org/10.4324/9780203959664

78. Holt, D. J., Cassidy, B. S., Andrews-Hanna, J. R., Lee, S. M., Coombs, G., Goff, D. C., Gabrieli, J. D., & Moran, J. M. (2010). An anterior-to-posterior shift in midline cortical activity in schizophrenia during self-reflection. *Biological Psychiatry, 69* (5), 415–423. https://doi.org/10.1016/j.biopsych.2010.10.003

79. Hope, N., Koestner, R., & Milyavskaya, M. (2014). The role of self-compassion in goal pursuit and well-being among university freshmen. *Self and Identity, 13*(5),

579–593. https://doi.org/10.1080/15298868.2014.889032

80. Inglehart, R., & Welzel, C. (2010). Changing mass priorities: The link between modernization and democracy. *Perspectives on Politics, 8*(2), 551–567. https://doi.org/10.1017/S1537592710001258

81. Iranzo-Bennett, R., Egan, H., Cook, A., & Mantzios, M. (2018). Mindfulness as an intervention for recalling information from a lecture as a measure of academic performance in higher education. *Higher Education for the Future, 5* (1), 75–88. https://doi.org/10.1177/2347631117738649

82. Irons, C., Gilbert, P., Baldwin, M. W., Baccus, J., & Palmes, M. (2006). Parental recall, attachment relating and self-attacking/self-reassurance: Their relationship with depression. *British Journal of Clinical Psychology, 45,* 297–308. https://doi.org/10.1348/014466505X68230

83. Jeffrey, D. L. (Ed.). (2007). *The Bible and the university* (Scripture and Hermeneutics Series). Paternoster/Zondervan Academic.

84. Jeste, D. V., & Vahia, I. V. (2008). Comparison of the conceptualization of wisdom in ancient Indian literature with modern views: Focus on the Bhagavad Gita. *Psychiatry, 71*(3), 197–209. https://doi.org/10.1521/psyc.2008.71.3.197

85. Judge, T. A., Bono, J. E., Ilies, R., & Gerhardt, M. W. (2002). Personality and leadership: A qualitative and quantitative review. *Journal of Applied Psychology, 87*(4), 765–780.

86. Kabat-Zinn, J. (1990). Full catastrophe living: Using the wisdom of your body and mind to face stress, pain, and illness. New York, NY: Delacorte Press.

87. Kao, Y.-C., Lien, Y.-J., Chang, H.-A., Tzeng, N.-S., Yeh, C.-B., & Loh, C.-H. (2017). Stigma resistance in stable schizophrenia: The relative contributions of stereotype endorsement, self-reflection, self-esteem, and coping styles. *The Canadian Journal of Psychiatry, 62*(10), 735–744. https://doi.org/10.1177/0706743717730827

88. Kapila, S. (2010). A history of violence. *Modern Intellectual History, 7*(2), 437–457. https://doi.org/10.1017/S1479244310000156

89. Kernis, M. H. (2003). Toward a conceptualization of optimal self-esteem. *Psychological Inquiry, 14*(1), 1–26. https://doi.org/10.1207/S15327965PLI1401_01

90. Kernis, M. H., & Goldman, B. M. (2006). A multicomponent conceptualization of authenticity: Theory and research. In M. Zanna (Ed.), *Advances in Experimental Social Psychology* (Vol. 38, pp. 283–357). Academic Press. https://doi.org/10.1016/S0065-2601(06)38006-9

91. Kernis, M. H., & Goldman, B. M. (2006). A multicomponent conceptualization of authenticity: Theory and research. In M. P. Zanna (Ed.), *Advances in Experimental Social Psychology* (Vol. 38, pp. 283–357). Academic Press.

92. Keyes, C. L. M., Shmotkin, D., & Ryff, C. D. (2002). Optimizing well-being: The empirical encounter of two traditions. *Journal of Personality and Social Psychology, 82*(6), 1007–1022. https://doi.org/10.1037/0022-3514.82.6.1007

93. Kierkegaard, S. (1954). *The sickness unto death* (W. Lowrie, Trans.). Doubleday. (Original work published 1849)

94. Krames, J. A. (2005). *Jack Welch and the 4 E's of leadership: How to put GE's leadership formula to work in your organization*. McGraw Hill.

95. Krishnamurti, J. (1953). *Education and the significance of life*. Harper & Brothers.

96. Kumari, S. (2019). Human Resilience in Great Indian Epic Mahabharata: A Study of Kavita Kane's Karna's Wife: The Outcast's Queen. *Journal of Advances and Scholarly Researches in Allied Education*, 16(4), 1930–1933.

97. Lambert, L. (1997). Constructivist leadership defined. *School Administration: The New Knowledge Base.*

98. Lazarus, R. S. (1966). *Psychological stress and the coping process*. McGraw-Hill.

99. Lazarus, R. S., & Folkman, S. (1984). *Stress, appraisal, and coping*. Springer Publishing Company.

100. LEE, Y. (2019). "He Xie" (Harmony) as Taoist statecraft in the *Tao Te Ching*. *SSRN Electronic Journal*. Elsevier. https://doi.org/10.2139/ssrn.3369324

101. Legate, N., Ryan, R. M., & Weinstein, N. (2012). Is coming out always a "good thing"? Exploring the relations of autonomy support, outness, and wellness for lesbian, gay, and bisexual individuals. *Social Psychological and Personality Science, 3*(2), 145–152. https://doi.org/10.1177/1948550611411929

102. Lenton, A. P., Bruder, M., Slabu, L., & Sedikides, C. (2013). How does "being real" feel? The experience of state authenticity. *Journal of Personality, 81*(3), 276–289. https://doi.org/10.1111/j.1467-6494.2012.00805.x

103. Levenson, M. R., Jennings, P. A., Aldwin, C. M., & Shiraishi, R. W. (2005). Self-transcendence:

Conceptualization and measurement. The International Journal of Aging and Human Development, 60(2), 127-143.

104. Lijtmaer, R. (2010). Reflections: Can the analyst share a traumatizing experience with a traumatized patient? *Psychodynamic Psychiatry, 38*(4), 685–692.

105. Lorenzen, D. N. (1999). Who invented Hinduism? *Comparative Studies in Society and History, 41*(4), 630–659. https://doi.org/10.1017/S0010417599003084

106. Lucas, R. E. (2007). Long-term disability is associated with lasting changes in subjective well-being: Evidence from two nationally representative longitudinal studies. *Journal of Personality and Social Psychology, 92*(4), 717–730. https://doi.org/10.1037/0022-3514.92.4.717

107. Lucas, R. E., & Donnellan, M. B. (2011). Estimating the reliability of single-item life satisfaction measures: Results from four national panel studies. *Social Indicators Research, 105*(3), 323-331. https://doi.org/10.1007/s11205-010-9773-5

108. Lucas, R. E., Clark, A. E., Georgellis, Y., & Diener, E. (2003). Reexamining adaptation and the set point model of happiness: Reactions to changes in marital status. *Journal of Personality and Social Psychology, 84*(3), 527–539. https://doi.org/10.1037/0022-3514.84.3.527

109. Lucas, R. E., Clark, A. E., Georgellis, Y., & Diener, E. (2004). Unemployment alters the set-point for life satisfaction. *Journal of Human Resources, 39*(2), 259–293.

110. Luechinger, S. (2009). Valuing air quality using the life satisfaction approach. *The Economic Journal, 119*(536), 482–515. https://doi.org/10.1111/j.1468-0297.2008.02241.x

111. Lykken, D., & Tellegen, A. (1996). Happiness is a stochastic phenomenon. *Psychological Science, 7*(3), 186–189. https://doi.org/10.1111/j.1467-9280.1996.tb00355.x

112. Magnus, K., Diener, E., Fujita, F., & Pavot, W. (1993). Extraversion and neuroticism as predictors of objective life events: A longitudinal analysis. *Journal of Personality and Social Psychology, 65*(5), 1046–1053.

113. Malakar, Y., Herington, M. J., & Sharma, V. (2019). The temporalities of energy justice: Examining India's energy policy paradox using non-western philosophy. *Energy Research and Social Science, 49*, 16–25. https://doi.org/10.1016/j.erss.2018.11.002

114. Mantzios, M., & Egan, H. (2019). An experiential reflection of a mindful lecturer: Exploring enhancement of active learning in higher education. *Higher Education Pedagogies, 4*(1), 194–207. https://doi.org/10.1080/23752696.2019.1601992

115. Mantzios, M., Egan, H., & Cook, A. (2019a). Mental Health First Aid for students in the health professions: Exploring opportunities for experiential learning in higher education. *Health Professions Education, 5*(4), 351–353.

116. Mantzios, M., Egan, H., & Cook, A. (2019b). Mental Health First Aid embedment within undergraduate psychology curriculums: An opportunity of applied experience for psychology students and for enhancing mental health care in Higher Education institutions. *Higher Education Pedagogies, 4*(1), 51–55.

117. Maslow, A. H. (1971). The farther reaches of human nature. New York, NY: Viking Press.

118. Masten, A. S. (2001). Ordinary magic: Resilience processes in development. *American Psychologist*, 56(3), 227–238. https://doi.org/10.1037/0003-066X.56.3.227

119. McCloskey, L. E. (2015). Mindfulness as an intervention for improving academic success among students with executive functioning disorders. *Procedia - Social and Behavioral Sciences, 174,* 221–226. https://doi.org/10.1016/j.sbspro.2015.01.650

120. Meichenbaum, D. (1985). Stress inoculation training. *Counseling Psychologist*, 13(4), 615–632. https://doi.org/10.1177/0011000085134006

121. Michalos, A. C. (1986). An application of multiple discrepancies theory to seniors. *Social Indicators Research, 18*(4), 349–373.

122. Mishra, R. (2024). Revisiting Indian Philosophy: A Study of Ethical Codes in Bhagwat Gita. *The SPL Journal of Literary Hermeneutics: A Biannual International Journal of Independent Critical Thinking*, *4*(1), 194-205.

123. Moffitt, J. (1977). The Bhagavad Gita as way-shower to the transcendental. *Theological Studies, 38*(2), 316-328. https://doi.org/10.1177/004056397703800204

124. Morgan, J., & Farsides, T. (2009). Measuring meaning in life. Journal of Happiness Studies, 10(2), 197-214.

125. Mulla, Z. R., & Krishnan, V. R. (2014). Karma-Yoga: The Indian model of moral development. *Journal of Business Ethics, 123*(2), 339–351. https://doi.org/10.1007/s10551-013-1842-8

126. Muniapan, B. (2016). Philosophy and management: The relevance of Vedanta in management. In *Managerial Strategies and Solutions for Business Success in Asia* (pp. 124–139). https://doi.org/10.4018/978-1-5225-1886-0.ch007

127. Muniapan, B., & Satpathy, B. (2013). The 'dharma' and 'karma' of CSR from the Bhagwad-Gita. *Journal of Human Values, 19* (2), 173–187. https://doi.org/10.1177/0971685813492265

128. Nagel, G. (1998). *Tao of teaching: Reflections on education and the Tao*. [Note: Verify exact publication details, as this may refer to Greta Nagel's work.]

129. Neff, K. D. (2003a). Self-compassion: An alternative conceptualization of a healthy attitude toward oneself. *Self and Identity, 2* (2), 85–101. https://doi.org/10.1080/15298860309032

130. Neff, K. D. (2003b). The development and validation of a scale to measure self-compassion. *Self and Identity, 2*(3), 223–250.https://doi.org/10.1080/15298860390209035

131. Neff, K. D. (2011). Self-compassion, self-esteem, and well-being. *Social and Personality Psychology Compass, 5*(1), 1–12.

132. Neff, K. D., & McGehee, P. (2010). Self-compassion and psychological resilience among adolescents and young adults. *Self and Identity, 9* (3), 225–240. https://doi.org/10.1080/15298860902979307

133. Neff, K. D., & McGehee, P. (2010). Self-compassion and psychological resilience among adolescents and young adults. *Self and Identity, 9* (3), 225–240.

134. Neff, K. D., Kirkpatrick, K. L., & Rude, S. S. (2007). Self-compassion and adaptive psychological functioning. *Journal of Research in Personality, 41*(1), 139–154. https://doi.org/10.1016/j.jrp.2006.03.004

135. Newman, D. S., Villarreal, J. N., Gerrard, M. K., McIntire, H., Barrett, C. A., & Kaiser, L. T. (2022). Deliberate practice of consultation communication

skills: A randomized controlled trial. *School Psychology, 37*(3), 225–235. https://doi.org/10.1037/spq0000494

136. Pande, N., & Naidu, R. K. (1992). Anāsakti and health: A study of non-attachment. *Psychology & Developing Societies, 4* (1), 89–104. https://doi.org/10.1177/097133369200400106

137. Pandey, A., & Mishra, P.C. (2021). Pursuit of resilience: A deep analysis in pages of Bhagavad Gita. *International Journal of Indian Psychology,* 9 (1), 527-531. DOI: 10.25215/0901.052

138. Pavot, W., & Diener, E. (1993). Review of the Satisfaction With Life Scale. *Psychological Assessment, 5*(2), 164–172. https://doi.org/10.1037/1040-3590.5.2.164

139. Pearce, C. L., & Conger, J. A. (Eds.). (2003). *Shared leadership: Reframing the hows and whys of leadership.* SAGE Publications.

140. Pepping, C. A., Davis, P. J., O'Donovan, A., & Pal, J. (2015). Individual differences in self-compassion: The role of attachment and experiences of parenting in childhood. *Self and Identity, 14* (1), 104–117. https://doi.org/10.1080/15298868.2014.955050

141. Petrides, K. V. (2011). Ability and trait emotional intelligence. In T. Chamorro-Premuzic, S. von Stumm, & A. Furnham (Eds.), *The Wiley-Blackwell handbook of individual differences* (pp. 656–678). Wiley-Blackwell.

142. Piedmont, R. L. (1999). Does spirituality represent the sixth factor of personality? Spiritual transcendence and the five-factor model. Journal of Personality, 67(6), 985-1013.

143. Pinquart, M., & Sörensen, S. (2000). Influences of socioeconomic status, social network, and competence

on subjective well-being in later life: A meta-analysis. *Psychology and Aging, 15* (2), 187–224.

144. Prasko, J., Mozny, P., Novotny, M., Slepecky, M., & Vyskocilova, J. (2012). Self-reflection in cognitive behavioural therapy and supervision. *Biomedical Papers, 156*(4), 377–384. https://doi.org/10.5507/bp.2012.027

145. Radhakrishnan, S. (1994). *The principal Upanishads.* HarperCollins India.

146. Ramos, A. C. (2017). Piecing together ideas on sociocultural psychology and methodological approaches. *Integrative Psychological and Behavioral Science, 51*(2), 279–284. https://doi.org/10.1007/s12124-017-9389-3

147. Ram-Prasad, C. (2013). Divine self, human self: The philosophy of being in two Gītā commentaries. In *Divine Self, Human Self: The Philosophy of Being in Two Gita Commentaries* (pp. 1–148).

148. Ramsburg, J. T., & Youmans, R. J. (2014). Meditation in the higher-education classroom: Meditation training improves student knowledge retention during lectures. *Mindfulness, 5,* 431–441. https://doi.org/10.1007/s12671-013-0199-5

149. Ranganathananda, S. (2021). *The message of the Bhagavad Gita in modern interpretation*. Advaita Ashrama.

150. Raque-Bogdan, T. L., Ericson, S. K., Jackson, J., Martin, H. M., & Bryan, N. A. (2011). Attachment and mental and physical health: Self-compassion and mattering as mediators. *Journal of Counseling Psychology, 58*(2), 272–278. https://doi.org/10.1037/a0023041

151. Reed, P. G. (1991). Toward a nursing theory of self-transcendence: Deductive reformulation using

developmental theories. Advances in Nursing Science, 13(4), 64-77.

152. Ryan, R. M., & Deci, E. L. (2000). Self-determination theory and the facilitation of intrinsic motivation, social development, and well-being. *American Psychologist, 55*(1), 68–78. https://doi.org/10.1037/0003-066X.55.1.68

153. Ryan, R. M., & Deci, E. L. (2004). Autonomy is no illusion: Self-determination theory and the empirical study of authenticity, awareness, and will. In J. Greenberg, S. L. Koole, & T. Pyszczynski (Eds.), *Handbook of Experimental Existential Psychology* (pp. 449–479). Guilford Press.

154. Ryan, R. M., & Deci, E. L. (2017). *Self-determination theory: Basic psychological needs in motivation, development, and wellness*. Guilford Press.

155. Ryan, R. M., & Lynch, J. H. (1989). Emotional autonomy versus detachment: Revisiting the vicissitudes of adolescence and young adulthood. *Child Development, 60*(2), 340–356. https://doi.org/10.2307/1130981

156. Ryan, R. M., Legate, N., Niemiec, C. P., & Deci, E. L. (2012). Beyond illusions and defense: Exploring the possibilities and limits of human autonomy and responsibility through self-determination theory. In P. R. Shaver & M. Mikulincer (Eds.), *Meaning, mortality, and choice: The social psychology of existential concerns* (pp. 215–233). American Psychological Association. https://doi.org/10.1037/13748-012

157. Ryff, C. D. (1989a). Happiness is everything, or is it? Explorations on the meaning of psychological well-being. *Journal of Personality and Social Psychology, 57*(6), 1069–1081. https://doi.org/10.1037/0022-3514.57.6.1069

158. Ryff, C. D. (1989b). Beyond Ponce de Leon and life satisfaction: New directions in quest of successful aging. *International Journal of Behavioral Development, 12*(1), 35–55. https://doi.org/10.1177/016502548901200102

159. Ryff, C. D. (1995). Psychological well-being in adult life. *Current Directions in Psychological Science, 4*(4), 99–104. https://doi.org/10.1111/1467-8721.ep10772395

160. Ryff, C. D., & Keyes, C. L. M. (1995). The structure of psychological well-being revisited. *Journal of Personality and Social Psychology, 69* (4), 719–727.

161. Salovey, P., & Mayer, J. D. (1990). Emotional intelligence. *Imagination, Cognition and Personality, 9* (3), 185–211.

162. Sandvik, E., Diener, E., & Seidlitz, L. (1993). Subjective well-being: The convergence and stability of self-report and non-self-report measures. *Journal of Personality, 61* (3), 317–342.

163. Sankheangaew, P. (2022). *Tao Te Ching*: The unity of moral and social action for peaceful life. *SSRN Electronic Journal*. Elsevier. https://doi.org/10.2139/ssrn.4298919

164. Saricaoglu, H., & Arslan, C. (2013). An investigation into psychological well-being levels of higher education students with respect to personality traits and self-compassion. *Educational Sciences: Theory & Practice, 13* (4), 2097–2104. https://doi.org/10.12738/estp.2013.4.1740

165. Sarma, D. S. (2020). *The Bhagavad Gita: A new interpretation for modern times*. Ganesan Publishers.

166. Schmutte, P. S., & Ryff, C. D. (1997). Personality and well-being: Reexamining methods and meanings. *Journal of Personality and Social Psychology, 73* (3), 549–559. https://doi.org/10.1037/0022-3514.73.3.549

167. Schneider, L., & Schimmack, U. (2009). Self-informant agreement in well-being ratings: A meta-analysis. *Social Indicators Research, 94* (3), 363–376.

168. Schwarz, N., & Strack, F. (1999). Reports of subjective well-being: Judgmental processes and their methodological implications. In D. Kahneman, E. Diener, & N. Schwarz (Eds.), *Well-being: The foundations of hedonic psychology* (pp. 61–84). Russell Sage Foundation.

169. Seligman, M. E. P., & Csikszentmihalyi, M. (2000). Positive psychology: An introduction. *American Psychologist, 55* (1), 5–14. https://doi.org/10.1037/0003-066X.55.1.5

170. Shapiro, S. L., Brown, K. W., Thoresen, C., & Plante, T. G. (2011). The moderation of mindfulness-based stress reduction effects by trait mindfulness: Results from a randomized controlled trial. *Journal of Clinical Psychology, 67* (3), 267–277. https://doi.org/10.1002/jclp.20761

171. Shapiro, S. L., Carlson, L. E., Astin, J. A., & Freedman, B. (2006). Mechanisms of mindfulness. *Journal of Clinical Psychology, 62* (3), 373–386.

172. Sheldon, K. M., Ryan, R. M., Rawsthorne, L. J., & Ilardi, B. (1997). Trait self and true self: Cross-role variation in the Big-Five personality traits and its relations with psychological authenticity and subjective well-being. *Journal of Personality and Social Psychology, 73* (6), 1380–1393. https://doi.org/10.1037/0022-3514.73.6.1380

173. Shepard, R. N. (1979). Psychological relations and psychophysical scales: On the status of 'direct' psychophysical measurement. *Journal of Mathematical Psychology, 19* (1), 1–17. https://doi.org/10.1016/0022-2496(79)90002-5

174. Shin, S. J., & Zhou, J. (2007). When is educational specialization heterogeneity related to creativity in research and development teams? Transformational leadership as a moderator. *Journal of Applied Psychology, 92*(6), 1709–1721.

175. Sim, I., Hwang, E., & Sin, B. (2020). A self-reflection program for smoking cessation in adolescents: A phenomenological study. *International Journal of Environmental Research and Public Health, 17*(3), 1085. https://doi.org/10.3390/ijerph17031085

176. Singh, A. K., Singh, S., & Singh, M. P. (2012). Bioethics: A new frontier of biological science. *Cellular and Molecular Biology, 58*(1), 110–114. https://doi.org/10.1170/T928

177. Sinha, C. (2023). Beyond dehumanized gender identity: Critical reflection on neuroscience, power relationships, and law. *Integrative Psychological and Behavioral Science, 58*(4), 1684–1703. https://doi.org/10.1007/s12124-023-09814-8

178. Sirois, F. M. (2014). Procrastination and stress: Exploring the role of self-compassion. *Self and Identity, 13*(2), 128–145. https://doi.org/10.1080/15298868.2013.763404

179. Sneed, J. R., & Whitbourne, S. K. (2003). Identity processing and self-consciousness in middle and later adulthood. *The Journals of Gerontology Series B: Psychological Sciences and Social Sciences, 58*(6), P313–P319. https://doi.org/10.1093/geronb/58.6.p313

180. Spendelow, J. S., & Butler, L. J. (2015). Reported positive and negative outcomes associated with a self-practice/self-reflection cognitive-behavioural therapy exercise for CBT trainees. *Psychotherapy Research, 26*(5), 602–611. https://doi.org/10.1080/10503307.2015.1058983

181. Stubbe, J. H., Posthuma, D., Boomsma, D. I., & de Geus, E. J. C. (2005). Heritability of life satisfaction in adults: A twin-family study. *Psychological Medicine, 35* (11), 1581–1588.

182. Suh, E. M., Diener, E., & Fujita, F. (1996). Events and subjective well-being: Only recent events matter. *Journal of Personality and Social Psychology, 70*(5), 1091–1102.

183. Suh, E. M., Diener, E., Oishi, S., & Triandis, H. C. (1998). The shifting basis of life satisfaction judgments across cultures: Emotions versus norms. *Journal of Personality and Social Psychology, 74* (2), 482–493.

184. Swami Adgadanand. (n.d.). *Srimad Bhagavad Gita: Yatharth Gita (Manav-Dharmashastra).* Shri Paramhans Swami Adgadanandji Ashram Trust. Retrieved from Shri Paramhans Swami Adgadanandji Ashram, Gangeshwar, India.

185. Takano, K., & Tanno, Y. (2009). Self-rumination, self-reflection, and depression: Self-rumination counteracts the adaptive effect of self-reflection. *Behaviour Research and Therapy, 47*(3), 260–264. https://doi.org/10.1016/j.brat.2008.12.008

186. Tamang, J. P., & Samuel, D. (2010). Dietary cultures and antiquity of fermented foods and beverages. In *Fermented Foods and Beverages of the World* (pp. 1–40). https://doi.org/10.1201/EBK1420094954-5

187. Tedeschi, R. G., & Calhoun, L. G. (1996). The posttraumatic growth inventory: Measuring the positive legacy of trauma. *Journal of Traumatic Stress*, 9 (3), 455–471. https://doi.org/10.1002/jts.2490090305

188. Tiuraniemi, J. (2011). Medical and psychology students' self-assessed communication skills: A pilot study. *Patient Education and Counseling, 82* (3), 361–364.

189. Tiuraniemi, J., Läärä, R., Kyrö, T., & Lindeman, S. (2010). Medical and psychology students' self-assessed communication skills: A pilot study. *Patient Education and Counseling, 83* (2), 152–157. https://doi.org/10.1016/j.pec.2010.05.013

190. Tornstam, L. (1999). Gerotranscendence: A developmental theory of positive aging. Journal of Aging Studies, 13(2), 183-200.

191. Trilling, L. (1971). *Sincerity and authenticity*. Harvard University Press.

192. Urry, H. L., Nitschke, J. B., Dolski, I., Jackson, D. C., Dalton, K. M., Mueller, C. J., Ryff, C. D., Singer, B. H., & Davidson, R. J. (2004). Making a life worth living: Neural correlates of well-being. *Psychological Science, 15* (6), 367–372.

193. Uysal, A., Lin, H. L., & Knee, C. R. (2010). The role of need satisfaction in self-concealment and well-being. *Personality and Social Psychology Bulletin, 36* (2), 187–199. https://doi.org/10.1177/0146167209354518

194. Veenhoven, R. (2005a). Inequality of happiness in nations.*Journal of Happiness Studies, 6* (4), 351–355.

195. Veenhoven, R. (2005b). Return of inequality in modern society? Test by dispersion of life-satisfaction across time and nations.*Journal of Happiness Studies, 6* (4), 457–487.

196. Walumbwa, F. O., Avolio, B. J., Gardner, W. L., Wernsing, T. S., & Peterson, S. J. (2008). Authentic leadership: Development and validation of a theory-based measure. *Journal of Management, 34* (1), 89–126.

197. Wang, G., Oh, I.-S., Courtright, S. H., & Colbert, A. E. (2011). Transformational leadership and performance across criteria and levels: A meta-analytic review of 25

years of research. *Group & Organization Management, 36* (2), 223–270.

198. Wang, S., Wang, V. S., & Zolotykh, L. G. (2023). The way of discursive cognition of the ancient Chinese treatise *Tao Te Ching* in Russia. *RUDN Journal of Studies in Literature and Journalism*, 28 (1), 79–91. https://doi.org/10.22363/2312-9220-2023-28-1-79-91

199. Wang, Y. (2019). A study of polysemy and multi-translation in *Tao Te Ching*. *Advances in Social Science, Education and Humanities Research*. Atlantis Press. https://doi.org/10.2991/iccessh-19.2019.251

200. Waterman, A. S. (1993). Two conceptions of happiness: Contrasts of personal expressiveness (eudaimonia) and hedonic enjoyment. *Journal of Personality and Social Psychology, 64* (4), 678–691. https://doi.org/10.1037/0022-3514.64.4.678

201. Weinstein, N., Legate, N., Ryan, W. S., Sedikides, C., & Cozzolino, P. J. (2017). Autonomy support for conflictual and stigmatized identities: Effects on ownership and psychological health. *Journal of Counseling Psychology, 64* (5), 584–599. https://doi.org/10.1037/cou0000224

202. Wiest, M., Schüz, B., Webster, N., & Wurm, S. (2011). Subjective well-being and mortality revisited: Differential effects of cognitive and emotional facets of well-being on mortality. *Health Psychology, 30* (6), 728–735.

203. World Values Survey Association. (n.d.). *World Values Survey Wave 7 (2017–2022)*. Retrieved from https://www.worldvaluessurvey.org

204. Wu, Y., Wang, C., He, X., Mao, L., & Zhang, L. (2010). Religious beliefs influence neural substrates of self-reflection in Tibetans. *Social Cognitive and Affective*

Neuroscience, 5(3), 324–331. https://doi.org/10.1093/scan/nsq016

205. Yalom, I. D. (1980). *Existential psychotherapy*. Basic Books.

206. Yap, S. C. Y., Anusic, I., & Lucas, R. E. (2012). Does personality moderate reaction and adaptation to major life events? Evidence from the British Household Panel Survey. *Journal of Research in Personality, 46* (5), 477–488.

207. Zaehner, R. C. (2023). *The Bhagavad Gita: The song of God retold in modern times*. Oxford University Press. References (APA 7)

208. Zhang, X., & Bartol, K. M. (2010). Linking empowering leadership and employee creativity: The influence of psychological empowerment, intrinsic motivation, and creative process engagement. *Academy of Management Journal, 53* (1), 107–128.